Endorse
Creation's C

"*Creation's Glorious Story* contains much food for contemplation. Overall, I found Dowidat's book to be a tight, lean, thought-provoking faith-nurturing read. Though I may not agree with every word, I really liked the approach and plausibility of the creationist argument. As a previous atheist—I wasn't open minded enough years ago to even read a work like this. However, I definitely have people in mind with whom I will share this once final copies are available!" (July 2010)

    _____ Beth Jacqmain, Forester, B.S, M.S. Forest Biology (Ecology), Auburn University Alabama. Member Forest Guild Society of American Foresters.

Dan Dowidat's creationism series is truth from the Bible and his heart. Besides teaching it in my church fellowship for many years, I am thankful *Creation's Glorious Story* is now also in writing to refer to as the need arises and to help me grow as a Christian. This message helps me to have victory in Jesus and I give copies to people that I meet on the bus, street, in the workplace, and to other American Indian people. Jesus told us to teach all nations to spread the word of God. (July 2010)

    _____ Diana Buckanaga
    Leach Lake Ojibway
    Minneapolis, Minnesota

CREATION'S GLORIOUS STORY

by Daniel P. Dowidat

Copyright © 2010 by Daniel P. Dowidat
2nd printing 2011
Published by TrueNorth Publishing
6901 Ives Ln. N.,
Maple Grove, MN 55369
www.truenorthpublishingdt.com
Manufactured by Book Printing Revolution, Minneapolis, MN 55401

Cover design and interior art: Cheryl Barr
Editing: Delores E. Topliff, Creative Design Services, www.delorestopliff.com

ISBN 978-0-9842291-2-3

Published in the United States of America

This book is lovingly dedicated to my wife, Lorayne, with appreciation for her gifts related to intricate flora and fauna countryside observations through the years

CONTENTS

AUTHENTIFICATION: Prelude – Chapter 4

SEVEN DAYS AND BEYOND: Chapters 5-12

8-15-2017

FOREWORD

Daniel P. Dowidat has a multi-faceted resumé as a soldier, forester, land surveyor, rural real estate appraiser, and long-time lover of God's creation. In his thirties, after encountering the reality of God as Creator of this world and the claims of Jesus Christ as God's Son, Dowidat accepted Him as his personal Savior. Greatly impacted, Dowidat completed a forestry degree and theology studies, ultimately becoming a speaker, writer and chaplain relating science and theology. He strongly believes in the Bible as God's infallible and necessary Operator's Manual for man, God's crowning creative achievement, to read and understand the principles by which He created and governs the world.

Dowidat is grateful for the teachings of Henry M. Morris, founder of the Institute for Creation Research, and Ian T. Taylor, the voice of the radio broadcast, *Creation Moments*. In addition, Fred Iglesia, friend and Professor at Northwestern College, St. Paul, Minnesota, has been a major encourager behind Dowidat writing *Creation's Glorious Story*. Dowidat adds original poetry to convey his personal joy in knowing God, inviting readers to gain greater understanding of Jesus Christ, the Creator of this world.

Delores E. Topliff, B.A., M.A., A.B.D.,
President of the Minnesota Christian Writers Guild, Editor,
Publisher, and Seminar and College Teacher.
www.delorestopliff.com www.truenorthpublishingdt.com

The Holy Scripture is the basis for *Creation's Glorious Story* combined with my major life experiences and facts learned. In this book, geology, science and theology meet together in an effort to bridge the gap sometimes perceived between them, other than by the usual explanations presented by pure scientists or theologians. I love both the outdoors and God's poetic writings in the Bible. Observing and learning about the combined forces of geology and theology in creating our world has strengthened my faith. May this book glorify God, our Creator, by revealing His visible beauty and message as seen in both nature and Scripture. While reading through these pages, may believers, unbelievers and skeptics find encouragement, inspiration and valuable food for thought. It is my prayer that this book will be a blessing to God and to His people.

Daniel P. Dowidat – Minneapolis, 2010

INTRODUCTION

"For the beauty of the earth, for the glories of the skies,"[1]
For the sparkling universe below, around, above us lies,
Leading onwards, upwards, toward our Creator through His Word.

Thoughtful investigation was pursued in writing *Creation's Glorious Story*. This book focuses on the physical creation of the world of nature that mankind holds so dear. It highlights the beauty and stark boldness of creation through the laws of nature put into place by our God, Creator of the universe. God's created masterpieces, illustrated with teachings from scientific studies, are connected to God's wisdom in the Bible, linking the glory of our Creator to what we see, hear, and experience around us daily. Through diligent study of science and theology, the beauty and truth of God's creation is revealed in the orderly account found in God's book of beginnings, "Genesis," and the following books of the Bible. Incorporated within this book are poetic writings and picturesque descriptions to complement the beauty of God's natural world as reflected in His Scriptural record.

In this manuscript, prophecies of old are interwoven with the words of Christ. Although much of this writing is gospel-oriented, portions describing earth's physical creative process also come from the scientific studies of reliable Christian and secular scientists in their respective fields of expertise. Those writings are further complemented by the writings of theologians, outdoorsmen, and those inspired by the beauties of our physical earth.

"For the Beauty of the Earth," Folliott S. Pierpoint 1835-1917.

This book is written to help mankind understand the importance of Holy Scripture. It is not intended to make us better scientists although hopefully, that also will be the inevitable outcome. God's eternal word leads us to life everlasting through His Son Jesus Christ. God's Word is like a road map leading us to the knowable mind of Christ in whom we can "live and breathe and have our being."

Creation's Glorious Story reveals the glory of God in both His natural and spiritual creation. This is written to help readers to love all that God has committed to mankind's dominion during our walk on this planet. Most importantly, may the Creator Himself be magnified for what He has done through giving us His Son as the key to mankind's salvation and sanctification. May this writing glorify our Triune God and Creator, Father, Son and Holy Spirit, Maker of all things, visible and invisible: The psalmist makes a declaration of faith to God in Psalms 119:105, "Your word is a lamp to my feet, and a light to my path."

Creation's Glorious Story is also for those who love the Creator and all that He has brought into existence that reaches our senses of sight, smell, touch, hearing, and beyond the visible into the invisible. This book is intended to provide a fulfillment of the hope and beauty shown in God's world as described in His poetic word, the Bible. May believers, unbelievers and skeptics alike be encouraged by the hope of God's glory as revealed in nature and the Bible passages presented. As you travel through these pages, look deeply into God's word through this keyhole to observe the light of God's truths and creative being clearly declared throughout His universe.

There is a beauty in the air, singing a song beyond compare.
At times its music we don't discern, amid the rush of man's concerns.
A song arises within the soul, much beyond what man controls.

The sounds of nature rise on high, sung by birds up in the sky.
Woods and fields heavy with dew, draw forth songs of feeding, too.
Warmed and fed by sun and rain, the earth feeds all it does maintain.

The song goes on to all who hear, God's love call rings loud and clear;
Hills and valleys, mountain peaks, wooded glades and flowering trees.
Songs of beauty are what we see God's love extends eternally.

The Biblical Basics*

Note: All biblical passages noted numerically with a superscript are for the purpose of exact referencing. They are not footnotes or endnotes.

THE FIRST DAY:

Genesis 1:1-5 [1]In the beginning God created the heavens and the earth. [2]The earth was formless and void, and darkness was over the surface of the deep, and the Spirit of God was moving over the surface of the waters. [3]Then God said, "Let there be light"; and there was light. [4]God saw that the light was good; and God separated the light from the darkness. [5]God called the light day, and the darkness He called night. And there was evening and there was morning, one day.

The Spirit of God moves over the surface of the deep. Light and darkness are delineated.

THE SECOND DAY:

Genesis 1:6-8 [6]Then God said, "Let there be an expanse in the midst of the waters, and let it separate the waters from the waters." [7]God made the expanse, and separated the waters which were below the expanse from the waters which were above the expanse; and it was so. [8]God called the expanse heaven. And there was evening and there was morning, a second day.

God separates the waters below from the waters above. The firmament is formed.

THE THIRD DAY:

Genesis 1:9-13 [9]Then God said, "Let the waters below the heavens be gathered into one place, and let the dry land appear"; and it was so. [10]God called the dry land earth, and the gathering of the waters He called seas; and God saw that it was good. [11]Then God said, "Let the earth sprout vegetation: plants yielding seed, and fruit trees on the earth bearing fruit after their kind with seed in them"; and it was so. [12]The earth brought forth vegetation, plants yielding seed after their kind, and trees bearing fruit with seed in them, after their kind; and God saw that it was good. [13]There was evening and there was morning, a third day.

God gathers the waters together forming seas. Dry land appears bringing forth vegetation. Plants yielding seeds along with fruit trees are created.

THE FOURTH DAY:

Genesis 1:14-19 [14]Then God said, "Let there be lights in the expanse of the heavens to separate the day from the night, and let them be for signs and for seasons and for days and years; [15]and let them be for lights in the expanse of the heavens to give light on the earth"; and it was so. [16]God made the two great lights, the greater light to govern the day, and the lesser light to govern the night; He made the stars also. [17]God placed them in the expanse of the heavens to give light on the earth, [18]and to govern the day and the night, and to separate the light from the darkness; and God saw that it was good. [19]There was evening and there was morning, a fourth day.

God creates the sun, moon and stars; all the heavenly lights.

Biblical Basics continued

THE FIFTH DAY:
Genesis 1:20-23 [20]Then God said, "Let the waters teem with swarms of living creatures, and let birds fly above the earth in the open expanse of the heavens." [21]God created the great sea monsters and every living creature that moves, with which the waters swarmed after their kind, and every winged bird after its kind; and God saw that it was good. [22]God blessed them, saying, "Be fruitful and multiply, and fill the waters in the seas, and let birds multiply on the earth." [23]There was evening and there was morning, a fifth day.

God creates all of the sea creatures and the birds of the air.

THE SIXTH DAY:
Genesis 1:24-31 [24]Then God said, "Let the earth bring forth living creatures after their kind: cattle and creeping things and beasts of the earth after their kind"; and it was so. [25]God made the beasts of the earth after their kind, and the cattle after their kind, and everything that creeps on the ground after its kind; and God saw that it was good. [26]Then God said, "Let Us make man in Our image, according to Our likeness; and let them rule over the fish of the sea and over the birds of the sky and over the cattle and over all the earth, and over every creeping thing that creeps on the earth." [27]God created man in His own image, in the image of God He created him; male and female He created them. [28]God blessed them; and God said to them, "Be fruitful and multiply, and fill the earth, and subdue it; and rule over the fish of the sea and over the birds of the sky and over every living thing that moves on the earth." [29]Then God said, "Behold, I have given you every plant yielding seed that is on the surface of all the earth, and every tree which has fruit yielding seed; it shall be food for you; [30]and to every beast of the earth and to every bird of the sky and to every thing that moves on the earth which has life, I have given every green plant for food"; and it was so. [31]God saw all that He had made, and behold, it was very good. And there was evening and there was morning, the sixth day.

God creates all of the beasts of the earth, the cattle and all of the creatures that creep upon the ground.

God makes man and woman in His likeness, the likeness of His Son, and possibly that of other heavenly hosts.

THE SEVENTH DAY:
Genesis 2:1-3 [1]Thus the heavens and the earth were completed, and all their hosts. [2]By the seventh day God completed His work which He had done, and He rested on the seventh day from all His work which He had done. [3]Then God blessed the seventh day and sanctified it, because in it He rested from all His work which God had created and made.

God completes His work and rests from all His labors, blessing and sanctifying this seventh day.

AUTHENTIFICATION
Prelude and Chapters 1–4

PRELUDE
IN THE BEGINNING, GOD...

Psalms 90:2, 'Before the mountains were born or You gave birth to the earth and the world, even from everlasting to everlasting, You are God."

Scope of This Study

The first eleven foundation chapters of Genesis are essential to understanding all subsequent books in the Bible. If belief in God is not presently established in your heart and mind, you may tend to question the validity of the entire Bible. This study begins with Genesis 1:1 and continues through Genesis chapter 11 to the life of Abraham. Up to that point some people describe the Bible as allegorical, or as folklore or even fiction. In this study I seek to validate and present sovereign God as the Creator of all that exists on earth and the heavens above. This includes life and all things, both visible and invisible. In the review process, scripture portions and examples from folklore and ancient writers are included as well as thoughts from modern creationists seen through the viewpoint of the science and theology God provided. May God put hunger in your heart to understand His ways and principles. As Proverbs 25:2 says, "It is the glory of God to conceal a matter, but the glory of kings is to search out a matter."

Overview

The first four chapters of *Creation's Glorious Story* previews the initial days of creation presented in the book of Genesis. These first four chapters are a source for contemplation in establishing a foundation of faith and credibility with God as Creator.

Chapters 5-12 discuss from theology and science the questions of who, what, why and when concerning our existence in God's universe displayed from the beginning until today. The historical mandates presented by God, through His holy covenants with mankind, are still in effect for us today. Perhaps God, in His mercy, will grant us the time necessary to herald the return of Christ to earth with a new growth of life replacing that decimated by mankind through time. May we look forward to fulfilling God's ancient covenants with humankind by caring for the earth, nurturing it and restoring it to its pristine beauty as we fruitfully multiply while God allows us to occupy until He returns.

Chapter 1 shows the interacting roles of the Father, Son and Holy Spirit Trinity in relationship with each other through the process of creation's first six days. On the seventh day when God rested from His labors, He said that creation was complete and "very good."

Chapter 2 considers some questions invented by the enemy in an attempt to confuse the human race regarding God's existence and powers. Attempts are made to nullify the beauty of God's creation by citing the depth and despair of human wisdom without giving credit to God, the Creator, for His beautiful and ordered work. This chapter reviews some theories concerning the creation of the universe and world, exposing their limitations when not acknowledging scientific findings and the Bible.

Chapters 3 and 4 discuss the value of linguistics and semantics in evaluating the accuracy of the Bible from comparative ancient writings in Hebrew with minimal reference to Greek. This linguistics and semantics portion draws largely on studies by linguistics expert, James Stambaugh, in articles noted, with references coming from his excellent article, "The days of creation: A semantic approach." His material solidifies the understanding that the Bible is the true, inspired and inerrant word of God.

Chapters 5–12 each properly discuss the marvelous events God completed on each specific day of creation:

5 - Light: Day One

6 - Waters separated: Day Two

7 - Dry land, vegetation: Day Three

8 - Sun, moon, and the heavenly lights: Day Four

9 - Sea creatures and birds: Day Five

10- Cattle, beasts, creeping things, mankind: Day Six

11- God's rest: Day Seven

12- Post-creation: Day Seven to Abraham

Chapter 12 covers the time from God's rest on Creation's Day Seven when he pronounced creation "very good," through the fall of mankind into sin. It includes the interim 1656 years from creation to Noah's flood and then on to the earth's division at Babel, the continental drift period and the birth of Abraham around 2000 BC.

Limitations of this study

No human being was present during creation. The only ones in attendance were God the Father, the Son and the Holy Spirit, plus at times, some, members of the heavenly host. The only written document we have for learning what occurred during creation is found in the inspired word of God, His Holy Bible. Besides God telling us what we need to know about creation through His revelations in the Bible, our knowledge is supplemented by many things developed by mankind. Therefore biological and geological observations obtained through telescopes, microscopes, computers and other inventions inspired by God but constructed by man's intellect enhance this study.

I am grateful that God permitted trained earth scientists to gather unbiased information providing untainted sources confirming our understanding today. God's love for all people and His desire that we understand his ways and principles are also visible in Deuteronomy 29:29, "The secret things belong to the LORD our God, but the things revealed belong to us and to our sons forever, that we may observe all the words of this law."

4

Chapter 1
MAJESTY! MAJESTY!
KINGDOM AUTHORITY!

¹In the year of King Uzziah's death I saw the Lord sitting on a throne, lofty and exalted, with the train of His robe filling the temple. ²Seraphim stood above Him, each having six wings: with two he covered his face, and with two he covered his feet, and with two he flew. ³And one called out to another and said, 'Holy, Holy, Holy, is the LORD of hosts, The whole earth is full of His glory.' ⁴And the foundations of the thresholds trembled at the voice of him who called out, while the temple was filling with smoke. ISAIAH 6:1-4

Then I heard something like the voice of a great multitude and like the sound of many waters and like the sound of mighty peals of thunder, saying, 'Hallelujah! For the Lord our God, the Almighty, reigns. REVELATION 19:6

And they sang the song of Moses, the bond-servant of God, and the song of the Lamb, saying, 'Great and marvelous are Your works, O Lord God, the Almighty; Righteous and true are Your ways, King of the nations! ⁴Who will not fear, O Lord, and glorify Your name? For You alone are holy.' REVELATION 15:3

Then I heard the voice of the Lord, saying, "Whom shall I send, and who will go for Us?' Then I said, "Here am I. Send me!" ISAIAH 6:8

The establishment of God's Sovereignty through the Trinity: Our Bible is the story of God (Elohim), the Creator. All things in the heavens and on earth were made by our Triune God: God the Father, in cooperation with God the Son, and God the Holy Spirit. In Christian circles today, these three entities are called the God-head or Holy Trinity. Let us examine this three-in-one entity through excerpts taken from both the Old and New Testaments. Genesis 1:1–2 says, "In the beginning God created the heavens and the earth. [2]The earth was formless and void, and darkness was over the surface of the deep, and the Spirit of God was moving over the surface of the waters." Briefly, these verses establish God the Father and the Holy Spirit present and involved in creation's beginning. These entities are separate but yet one in the Godhead.'"

The following scriptures also reveal a relationship between the spirit of God and the Holy Spirit: John 4:24, "God is spirit, and those who worship Him must worship in spirit and truth." Here Jesus highlights the Spirit's relationship to God the Father. In John 15:26, He says, "When the Helper comes, whom I will send to you from the Father, *that is* the Spirit of truth who proceeds from the Father, He will testify about Me."

Though I am not expert in the Greek or Hebrew languages (except for the use of a good Bible concordance) and cannot always theologically differentiate between the word Spirit capitalized compared to when it is written lower case, scholars of old did make this distinction. Through the distinction of upper and lower case spellings in the Old and New Testament, we generally understand that when the word Spirit is capitalized, most theologians are comfortable that it indicates the Holy Spirit. However, the use of lower case consistently seems to indicate *spirit* in general, not indicating the Holy Spirit.

Some may ask, "Where does Jesus enter into the equation?" Consider the opening verses of John where Jesus (the Word) enters into creation with the Father–John 1:3: [1]"In the beginning was the Word, and the Word was with God, and the Word was God. [2]He was in the beginning with God. [3]All things came into being through Him, and apart from Him nothing came into being that has come into being." In the following passages the relationship of Jesus to God the Father is seen as separate, and yet one. John 17:20–21: [20]"'I do not ask on behalf of these alone, but for those also who believe in Me through their word; [21]that they may all be one; even as You, Father, *are* in Me and I in You, that they also may be in Us, so that the world may believe that You sent Me.'"

Further support is given by the Apostle Paul in Colossians 1:16–17 as he describes Christ's role in creation: [16]"For by Him all things were created, *both* in the heavens and on earth, visible and invisible, whether thrones or dominions or rulers or authorities—all things have been created through Him and for Him. [17]He is before all things, and in Him all things hold together." These New Testament passages establish Christ at the scene of creation with the Father. Scriptural sources from both the Old and New Testaments clearly show all three entities of the Godhead, God the Father, Son and Holy Spirit, involved in the creation.

The eternality of the Holy Trinity: God is eternal and so is His Son. We read in Romans 16:26, "but now is manifested, and by the Scriptures of the prophets, according

7

to the commandment of the eternal God." This eternal God, consisting of Father, Son and Holy Spirit, is also revealed in Revelation 22:13, which says, "I am the Alpha and the Omega, the first and the last, the beginning and the end." This statement made by Jesus speaks of Himself within the Godhead of the Holy Trinity. In contrast, an Old Testament verse in Isaiah 44:6 foreshadows Christ, by saying, "Thus says the LORD, the King of Israel and his Redeemer, the LORD of hosts: 'I am the first and I am the last, And there is no God besides Me.'" This earlier prophetic scripture refers to God the Father and the anticipated Christ within the Holy Trinity. Before anything was made, Jesus coexisted with His Father. Isaiah 9:6 goes on to prophesy of Christ referring to His eternality with the Eternal Father: "For a child will be born to us, a son will be given to us; And the government will rest on His shoulders; And His name will be called Wonderful Counselor, Mighty God, Eternal Father, Prince of Peace."

Some people describe Christ as being the firstborn of creation indicating that He did have a beginning but no ending. However, some sects and cults try to make this matter a foggy issue to shake the belief system of Christians regarding the eternality of the Holy Trinity before and after creation. Yet, the most important issue in the Bible is clearly addressed by the Apostle Paul: 1 Corinthians 15:3-4: "[3]For I delivered to you as of first importance what I also received, that Christ died for our sins according to the Scriptures, [4]and that He was buried, and that He was raised on the third day according to the Scriptures." It is not the Bible's purpose to be a history book or scientific text. Instead it is written to provide spiritual instruction and understanding, bringing

8

peace. Sadly, some sects twist insignificant portions of scripture that few truly understand to confuse or mislead kingdom seekers, like using smoke to darken mirrors.

The Bible's statement that Jesus is *the firstborn* means that He was sent from heaven by the Father to be born as a human among us so that He might become our Savior and effective older brother life example. In spite of being without sin, He paid our sin penalty in redemptive sacrifice and entered God's eternal rest Himself, and made the way for us, His redeemed brethren, who believe in His redemptive act. Prior to Jesus meeting all sin penalty requirements, mankind lacked the means to return to the Father. But at Calvary, Jesus established the way through obedience unto death on the cross, followed by His burial, resurrection in an incorruptible body, and ascension into heaven in exact fulfillment of numerous Old Testament prophecies.

Conceivably, Jesus Christ was initially created by God, or perhaps was in existence with Him from the beginning. Psalm 90:2, Isaiah 9:6, and Hebrews 1:1-12, are all passages implying that Jesus equally exists from everlasting to everlasting and describe His involvement with God the Father during the creation process. Psalms 90:2 says, "Before the mountains were born Or You gave birth to the earth and the world, even from everlasting to everlasting, You are God."

Further mention of the Son in the Godhead is found in Old Testament Psalms and the LXX Qumran text. (Note: The Qumran text is one of the Dead Sea Scrolls found in Israel in 1948. After 1948, this text dates back to around 150 B.C. and is remarkable in confirming faith because of its almost identical accuracy to the Isaiah text transmitted to us today.)

These same thoughts are spoken again in Hebrews 1:1-12 where they are separated from the New Testament writings by capital letters to indicate the Old Testament or Qumran root sources. These designated passages in Hebrews 1 are further followed in parenthesis by their Old Testament or Qumran sources of origin: [1]"God, after He spoke long ago to the fathers in the prophets in many portions and in many ways, [2]in these last days has spoken to us in His Son, whom He appointed heir of all things, through whom also He made the world. [3]And He is the radiance of His glory and the exact representation of His nature, and upholds all things by the word of His power. When He had made purification of sins, He sat down at the right hand of the Majesty on high, [4]having become as much better than the angels, as He has inherited a more excellent name than they. [5]For to which of the angels did He ever say, 'YOU ARE MY SON, TODAY I HAVE BEGOTTEN YOU'? (PSALMS 2:7). "And again read, 'I WILL BE A FATHER TO HIM AND HE SHALL BE A SON TO ME," (2 Samuel 7:14, referring to all the descendants of David. Here I believe it applies to Christ.) [6]"And when He again brings the firstborn into the world, He says 'AND LET ALL THE ANGELS OF GOD WORSHIP HIM.'" (Deuteronomy 32:43 in the LXX Qumran text is not in our interpretation of today's Bible usage.) [7]"And of the angels He says, 'WHO MAKES HIS ANGELS WINDS, AND HIS MINISTERS A FLAME OF FIRE.'" (Psalms 104:4); [8]"But of the Son *He says*, 'YOUR THRONE, O GOD, IS FOREVER AND EVER, AND THE RIGHTEOUS SCEPTER IS THE SCEPTER OF HIS KINGDOM. (Psalms 45:6) [9]"YOU HAVE LOVED RIGHTEOUSNESS AND HATED LAWLESSNESS; THEREFORE GOD, YOUR GOD, HAS ANOINTED YOU WITH THE OIL OF GLADNESS ABOVE YOUR COMPANIONS." (Psalms 45:7); [10]"And, 'YOU, LORD, IN THE BEGINNING LAID THE

FOUNDATION OF THE EARTH, AND THE HEAVENS ARE THE WORKS OF YOUR HANDS; (Psalms 102:25); [11]THEY WILL PERISH, BUT YOU REMAIN; AND THEY ALL WILL BECOME OLD LIKE A GARMENT, (Psalms 102:26); [12]AND LIKE A MANTLE YOU WILL ROLL THEM UP; LIKE A GARMENT THEY WILL ALSO BE CHANGED. BUT YOU ARE THE SAME, AND YOUR YEARS WILL NOT COME TO AN END." (Psalms 102:27).

A summary of Hebrews 1:1-12 states that Jesus, as the Creator of the heavens and earth, is the culmination of all Old Testament prophecies and the perfect human representation of Holy God in His glory. Christ is God's firstborn Son appointed above all peoples and principalities in heaven and in the earth. As God's Son He chose to honor His Father through total obedience and righteousness, cleansing the world of sin for our sakes to restore us to the Father. Therefore, He now sits in heaven on the right hand of the throne of God to live and reign forever, making room for us to join Him in the restored family or "Household of God."

In the popular Rogers and Hammerstein musical, *The Sound of Music,* the composers have Julie Andrews as Maria sing, "Nothing comes from nothing, nothing ever could." Albert Einstein, winner of the 1921 Nobel prize-winner in physics, presented the theorem, "Matter, can neither be created or destroyed." Yet neither of these statements goes beyond the initial creation process of our supernatural God of all creation. His majestic creation of something from nothing through His miraculous powers shown throughout the Bible, are stated in His following Scriptures: Romans 4:17 says, (as it is written, "A FATHER OF MANY NATIONS HAVE I MADE YOU") in the presence of Him whom he believed, *even* God, who gives life to the dead and calls into being that which does not exist. It is echoed again in Hebrews 11:3, "By faith we understand that the worlds were prepared by the word of God, so that what is seen was not made out of things which are visible."

Two Hebrew words are used to mean create, these are *bara*, *asah* and another similar word, *yatsar*, meaning "formed." The first, *Bara*, is only used as create when describing an act of God. The significance of this is that only God can create something from nothing as expressed through this Old Testament usage.

The other Hebrew word used for create is *Asah*, sometimes used interchangeably with *bara*, but most often used when it means created from something already in existence. Finally, *Yatsar*, normally means formed, as in God formed man out of the dust of the ground. I've included this word because of its implication of *shaping* by God.

As much as is humanly possible, everything included in this study is scripturally-based and supported by books and commentaries penned by theological experts. When scripture does not address an issue directly, the most likely interpretation is chosen. If scripture does not clearly comment on an issue, its overall biblical importance is considered low.

In studying the miraculous first eleven chapters of Genesis, much rich supplemental information is provided from scientific fields to complement the biblical record. Studies by highly respected scientists and theologians are combined and included to help establish logical sequence for the marvelous events surrounding the creation wonders that we see on earth today. It is important to biblically establish the position of the entity of the Godhead consisting of Father, Son, and Holy Spirit as the Creator described in the preceding chapters 1-4 in order to intelligently describe the act of creation described in Genesis 1-11 and followed in Creation's Glorious Story, chapters 5-12. The role of the Trinitarian Creator is paramount to logical understanding of His cooperative role in the lives of men throughout the earth and universe enjoyed by us in both biblical and scientific records today:

The Alpha and Omega are one,
Consisting of the Father, Spirit and Son.
Creator of everything visible we see,
Stretching beyond our senses eternally.

In the beginning of earth, sky and sea,
The Godhead provided for you and me,
Seascapes, landscapes the heavens above,
Provided for all the creatures He loves.

The best things in life are free,
Available to all who touch, hear, or see.
The glory of God is there to behold;
The beauty of nature is not to be sold.

His beauty and love reign forever on high,
Extended to all now destined to die.
We can live forever with Him, we're told;
When within our lives His free gift unfolds.

Chapter 2

THEORIES OF CREATION

For since the creation of the world His invisible attributes, His eternal power and divine nature, have been clearly seen, being understood through what has been made, so that they are without excuse. ROMANS 1:20

Biblical Creation

Concerning creation, just what is a person supposed to believe? Ancient myths and folklore? Buddhism? Hinduism? New Age? Science? Cultic fiction? Atheism? The Biblical account? As scripture says in 2 Corinthians 2:9-10, "the mind of man cannot conceive of the glories that God has prepared for those who love Him."

Christians believe in God, the Father, as the Creator working in cooperative partnership with the two other parts of the Trinity, Christ, and the Holy Spirit. Our basis for this belief is God's word, the Bible. Let us examine the biblical account of creation along with some conflicting views put forward by atheistic evolutionists, which some misdirected

Creation's Glorious Story

Christians and other cultic or New Age type groups may believe: 2 Peter 1:20-21, "But know this first of all, that no prophecy of Scripture is a *matter* of one's own interpretation, [21]for no prophecy was ever made by an act of human will, but men moved by the Holy Spirit spoke from God."

God created man in His own image as a creative, inquisitive, and thinking being. Therefore he is capable of unraveling the many mysteries of the universe, nature's earth, and even into the deep recesses of our minds and souls. I believe that God is gladdened by man's discoveries of the riches in God's established order throughout the extensive reaches of our environment. God's laws are natural, but also social. Nearly all of mankind's scientific discoveries and inventions result from the stability of God's created laws. Non-Christian scientific discoveries, whether natural or social, seldom benefit mankind in general. However, God is sovereign. He is not restricted by the laws He has set in motion and at times He miraculously acts beyond normal limitation.

The ordered conformity, distribution and size of the heavenly bodies throughout the universe all indicate a Creator using intelligent design. For example, we do not find a large number of stars crowded into one small portion of the heavens while the remaining stars are scattered randomly across relatively vast empty areas. Instead we find order throughout the vast realm that we humans measure. Some stars, planets, moons and asteroids are much smaller or larger than others as seen from human viewpoints and based on factors like where we live or how we observe nature and the universe. However, when viewing the heavens, we find no unusually dominating sizes. They all seem to fall visibly within a range that we as humans can measure. Their ordered pattern indicates that they were established according to the designed plan of God, their Creator. In Psalms 8:3, the Bible speaks of the individual placement of all heavenly bodies: "When I consider Your heavens, the work of Your fingers, The moon and the stars, which You have ordained;" Also consider Job 9:7-9: [7]"It is God...who sets a seal upon the stars;... [8]who alone stretches out the heavens... [9]who makes the Bear, Orion and the Pleiades, and the chambers of the south;" In addition, read Isaiah 40:26,"Lift up your eyes on high and see who has created these *stars,* the One who leads forth their host by number, He calls them all by name; because of the greatness of His might and the strength of *His* power, not one *of them* is missing."

Some scientists explain the intensity of the stars through the explanation of an expanding universe and its varying measured speeds. However, God's creation is not limited by the speed of light. Scientists reveal that what we see, hear and understand of the heavens is actually a very small range of perception compared to all of the different rays that exist. There are rays both so short and so long that they are beyond human perception, yet scientists know that they exist and use them in scientific investigations. Short rays, like X-rays, are used in medicine and adapted by technology to be projected onto a screen to make them visible to our eyes. Similarly, long radio waves beyond human hearing perception are also used by astronomers in their investigations of the universe.

Contrary to the scientific theory of a uniformly expanding universe, stars do differ in light intensity when determined as equal distances from the earth. The Bible says of this phenomenon: "There is one glory of the sun, and another glory of the moon, and another glory of the stars; for star differs from star in glory." (1 Corinthians 15:41)

All that we see, touch, taste, hear, and experience in our very bodies, as well as throughout the universe, reinforces our belief in cosmic intelligent design and its inspired Designer. Even atheistic evolutionists cannot acknowledge that everything that we see around us has come about through chance. They cannot propose that if you took a watch apart and placed its loose parts in a bag and shook that bag for five billion years that all of the parts would recombine to form a perfect and complete watch. When we look at an architecturally-designed building, we may wonder who conceived of the plan and built it. We do not assume that no one did, that it simply assembled itself. We are certain that behind the visible structure, we are seeing the combined efforts of an architect, contractor and many professional workmen all working together in its construction. Is it not equally understandable that someone of marvelous intelligence created the design and details of the individual human body as well as our incomprehensibly complex vast universe?

One moonlit night, God gave me a personal revelation that defies human understanding. As I stood outside looking up into the starry sky, I saw the moon in its monthly phases. I suddenly realized that the placement and orbits of the moon, sun and earth in the heavens are so exact that there had to be an all-wise Creator involved with their placement and plan. It is all far too exact to have come about through chance.

The same consistent and perfect order is visible when

we observe eclipses of the sun or moon. When the earth eclipses the moon, it does so perfectly, just like a penny covers over a penny. When the moon eclipses the sun it is also perfect, again like a penny covering over a penny. If the placement of these heavenly bodies in our solar system were accomplished by chance, wouldn't these eclipses at least occasionally overlap one another like a dime crossing over a half-dollar, or a quarter over a penny? The fact that this does not happen indicates the perfect individual placement of the heavenly bodies by the grand Designer, God our Creator.

Romans 1:18-20 confirms the understanding given to me on that outstanding evening—and provides a wake-up call to salvation through presenting accompanying precise and observable scientific facts: "[18]For the wrath of God is revealed from heaven against all ungodliness and unrighteousness of men who suppress the truth in unrighteousness, [19]because that which is known about God is evident within them; for God made it evident to them. [20]For since the creation of the world His invisible attributes, His eternal power and divine nature, have been clearly seen, being understood through what has been made, so that they are without excuse." I believe that the personal revelation God gave me that night is common to those who will perish unless they listen to God and heed His direction.

The Big Bang Theory of Beginnings is a non-biblical explanation of beginnings and the starry universe. According to the *Big Bang Theory*, massive amounts of matter were all gathered in one place in darkened space at the time of our solar system's beginning. Suddenly for no apparent reason the matter powerfully exploded, scattering globs across the known universe in the form of hot burning gaseous elements and molten rocks mixed with all other elements known to man. Next these individual hot fluid globs were set to spinning, eventually forming spheres identifiable today as the earth, sun, moon, planets, asteroids and stars, along with other related heavenly bodies. All of these glowing globs traveled at different rates of speed, therefore creating differing light intensities. Faster-moving bodies produced lower intensity light than the slower moving ones due to their advanced light years of speed.

This can be compared to the high-intensity sound of an approaching plane that is followed by noticeably changing sounds in lower tones as the plane reaches us, and then changes again as it begins moving away from us and sound waves lengthen. The theory of an expanding universe is essential to The Big Bang Theory since its endorsers explain the universe as expanding at a rapid rate that one day reached maximum distance and then began collapsing on itself, only to repeat the action and eventually start a Big Bang process all over again. Supposedly, the Big Bang sequence producing our solar system occurred four to five billion years ago.

When these globs of spinning elements cooled, Big Bang exponents theorize that crystallized molten rock and liquid chemical seas were created. These chemical seas or *element soup*, (my term, and described fully in Chapter 7), became the *primeval ooze* (biological evolutionary term), from which they propose that all of life evolved by chance. According to that explanation, those chemicals combined over billions of years to become alive and evolve into all life forms known today. Frankly, believing that explanation requires a considerable amount of faith. But, faith in who, or what? In a reliable ordered source? You've got to be kidding. I've put my faith in God as Creator of the universe who interacts with me through a satisfying and loving father-son relationship.

Years ago when I possessed little wisdom concerning the Bible or God, I was led astray by upper echelon non-Christian educators to wonder if God used the Big Bang to create. For a while I made the assumption that if a great mass of matter exploded from one central location, all resulting heavenly lights would be visible from Day One, while expanding in outward patterns across space and time as explained by theorists. However, that possibility does not mesh with observed reality today concerning all of the starry hosts of the universe, even while they are at arithmetically impossible distances away in measured light years.

Neither could I believe in the theory of life as evolving from primeval ooze. Although while in college training, I once believed in an old-earth of four to five billion years of age, I now believe that God created all life as stated in the Bible and in the same sequence given there. My college historical geology class taught that our earth is the same now as it has always been, and that all natural rock formations and sequences existing today are the same as those existing in past millenniums. Evolutionists teach an age-old earth explanation because they need that much passage of time to justify their theories. However, they do not take into account the results of some very simple and basic experiments in physics, chemistry, natural observations, historical biblical information, and the sovereignty of a personal God capable of conceiving a different approach, beyond the mind of man, to govern nature according to the laws He set in motion.

The Gap Theory of Creation:

Thoughts of the Creationists: *We don't believe it!*
Thoughts of the Scientific Evolutionists: *They don't believe it either!*

The Gap Theory is believed by various cults as well as by some uninformed Christians. *Wikipedia* defines it this way: "Gap creationism (also known as Ruin-Restoration creationism, Restoration creationism, or "The Gap Theory"), is a form of Old Earth creationsim that posits that the six-day creation, as described in the Book of Genesis involved literal 24-hour days, but that there was a gap of time between two distinct creations in the first and the second verses of Genesis, explaining many scientific observations, including the age of the earth. In this it differs from Day-Age creationsim, which states that the 'days' of creation were then much longer periods (of thousands or millions of years), and from young earth creationsim, which although it agrees concerning the six literal 24-hour days of creation, does not posit any gap of time."

In simpler terms, the Gap Theory is basically a belief that there was an initial divine creation where mankind and all living things were formed as explained in Genesis, but that some kind of devastating destruction then took place between Genesis 1:1 and 1:2 which lasted billions of years with different geological formations resulting to produce what we see in earth's geological record today.

Exponents of this theory believe that the fluid nature

of the earth's core broke through its crust causing great upheaval of molten material to form magma-based mountain ranges with their characteristic igneous rocks of granites and associated mineral deposits. Other igneous surface deposits also resulted with volcanic lava flows creating basalts, obsidians and various other surface-originating rocks.

At that same time, extensive marine deposits formed beds of sedimentary rock formations of limestone, sandstone and shale throughout the world. These suggest that fluctuations of the earth's crust caused the seas to rise and fall, adding depth to new formations above the first rocks formed. This overburden of rock and water applied great heat and pressure to lower rock formations, transforming them into metamorphic rocks.

While still holding their original identity, these transformed metamorphic rocks were internally changed. One such example is marble as the final product made from far softer limestone through the metamorphic process. This explanation of rock formation and process is accepted by most geologists today. While I concur with their basic belief in terms of the sequence of rock formations, I do not accept their explanation that billions of years were necessary for this to occur. Their theory reflects a misunderstanding of the Genesis record:

Genesis 1:1, "In the beginning God created the heavens and the earth." Genesis 1:2a "The earth was formless and void, and darkness was over the surface of the deep..." Many non-believing groups use this scripture to misguide Christians or seekers by stating that the first verse indicates the first creation only. They describe that creation as containing all of the life forms that we see today in the geological rock record that took many ages to form. They say that after the heavens and earth had existed for unknown ages, unexplained chaos occurred in verse 2, bringing darkness throughout the universe and making the earth formless and void.

Other groups teach that the chaos in the universe was caused by God and Satan having a great cosmic battle over who had supremacy. We know that God is sovereign and rules over all that He has created, including Lucifer, who fell to become Satan, and Lucifer's followers. Some points wrong with the cosmic battle concept is that it represents Satan as having power nearly equal with God, which is untrue and contradicts God's Word. According to the Bible, Satan was a beautiful created being who rebelled against God rather than submit to His divine authority. As a result, Satan fell away from beauty and order into depravity and destructive chaos. As stated in the Bible, God's qualities are unique to Himself and His Son. Nowhere in scripture are those qualities imputed to any other man, angel, or fallen angel once blessed by God. All life is subject to God, including those angelic beings currently living in heaven in grace, as well as the fallen one-third of angels under Satan's sway.

Genesis 1:2b: "and the Spirit of God was moving over the surface of the waters. ³Then God said, 'Let there be light'; and there was light." Here the creation story resumes. Light and life were restored by the God of the universe, leaving in place the geological record in the first creation. This explains the phenomenon of the life recorded in rock formations which complies with an age old earth age of four to five billion years. This line of thinking has been impressed upon a gullible public by many college professors attempting to explain creation through the theory of evolution while excluding God's involvement.

The Gap Theory is an attempt at compromise between those believing in divine creationism and those embracing evolution. Whether they accept God as the original Creator or line up with evolutionists, a person can believe in the Gap Theory. However, the problem with it is that it is not fully logical or satisfyingly believable to either creationists or evolutionists. Young earth creationists explain creation as occurring during six 24-hour days. Those believing in evolution and an age-old earth maintain that formation of the earth continued through theorized chaos and darkness throughout the projected billions of years that this explanation requires.

God's account of creation is revealed in the Bible by Moses and inspired prophets. Now let me add comments derived from respected Christian and secular books, as well as my own experience and understanding gained while living on this earth and enjoying the presence of and awareness of God. Genesis 1:2 explains, "The earth was formless and void, and darkness was over the surface of the deep, and the Spirit of God was moving over the surface of the waters." This scripture indicates that God created all matter prior to the creation of the earth. The terms "formless, void, darkness and deep," seem to indicate pre-creation condition of the universe prior to the six-day creation of the heavens and earth as we know it. The narration concerning God's Spirit moving over the surface of the waters also indicates His existence prior to the six-day creation account. In Hebrew, *rachaph*, the word used for "moved," means a vacillating, vibrating movement not inconsistent with secular theories concerning origins of wave and particle movements on a micro-scale in quantum physics. Well-known creationist, Henry Morris, identified the word *rachaph* as also interpreted "shake and flutter" in both Jeremiah 23:9 and Deuteronomy 32:11.

This vacillating movement may be the methodology that God used to bring an inert universe to life. Also, use of the word "waters" makes it appear that this matter, created by God, was of a liquid nature, possibly water within an element mix. No matter how you look at it, and whatever the mix, all of earth and the starry hosts are composed of it. This is supported in 2 Peter 3:5 which explains, "...and *the* earth was formed out of water and by water." Similarly Genesis 1:1 states, "In the beginning God created the heavens and the earth." This does not mean that they were created at the same time in Day One. Instead, I believe the biblical record indicates that light was created on Day One, but that the heavens, containing all matter, were created previously. Scriptural support for this thinking is found in: 2 Peter 3:5, "it escapes their notice that by the word of God *the* heavens existed long ago and *the* earth was formed out of water and by water." My comprehension of this is that the heavens, which I understand to mean the basic matter of the universe, existed prior to the earth's formation. If that were not the case, why would Peter not have explained that the heavens 'and earth' existed long ago, thereby including them in the same grammatical time frame. Since he did not, I believe he was inspired to convey that the makings of the universe were already in place prior to the earth's formation. God may have called all matter into existence, including a roughed-out earth and universe, prior to His six creation days. I believe this view is consistent with both Genesis 1 and 2 Peter 3:5. In addition, notice that in Genesis, each day of God's creation begins with the word, "Let." For Day One God only says: "Let there be light." The other five days of creation give more detail on the ensuing process. This implies that the actual physical formation of the earth, sky and seas were all formed with their life during the five days after Creation's Day One. However, light in this case is not that of the sun, moon and stars, but seemingly a separate light, perhaps like an aurora, maybe emanating from God Himself or ordained by Him in the pre-formed universe.

The master engineer of all eternity may have been in the planning process not only concerning creation of the earth, but the total universe that we presently see partially displayed in the starry sky visible above us. How long might such planning have taken? Since God is omnipotent and omniscient, all of creation as we know it could have occurred within the span of a single day to include the creation of all basic matter and planet earth. Or He may previously have taken a large amount of eternity to plan and prepare creation. God is eternal with no beginning or end, from everlasting to everlasting. He is the Creator of everything around us, seen and unseen. For most of early eternity, He may have been creatively planning the establishment of His universe and all life within it, the greatest engineering feat known to man and angels. Considering God's infinitely creative nature and His brilliant loving plan to create man and his helpmeet to care for the Garden of Eden, it is understandable that God was not idle during the time span preceding His creation of the earth and the starry host of the heavens.

The biblical beauty of a Grand Designer creating our universe through purposeful creative acts as seen in Holy Scripture far exceeds evolution's stark explanation. Similarly, the hope extended through God as a Creator desiring personal relationship with mankind stands in sharp contrast to a hopeless and impersonal universe omitting the benevolent God visibly seen in the Bible and in nature. His inspiring design, patterns and poetic expressions help us to see and know His eternal divine qualities. They also establish and underscore His invitation to draw us from hopeless lives and destiny into a realm filled with His light and wisdom into a rich relationship with Him as presented in God's holy book, the Bible:

> The Creator is there to redeem,
> His love to mankind is readily seen.
> Attached to each vision are lives lived in freedom,
> Readily available to all in God's kingdom.
>
> We see God's gift to mankind,
> His creation of nature by design,
> Made for Him to give our life on earth
> To His glory with thanks for the second birth.

Chapter 3
CREATION'S DAY:
LINGUISTICS AND SEMANTICS

But know this first of all, that no prophecy of Scripture is a matter of one's own interpretation, for no prophecy was ever made by an act of human will, but men moved by the Holy Spirit spoke from God. 2 PETER 1:20-21

Chapters 1 and 2 discussed establishment of the Godhead as the Creator of all that we know on earth as well as in the visible and invisible universe. Linguistics and semantics are now used in chapters 3 and 4 to increase accurate understanding of the role of inspired writing in Genesis 1 and 2 pertaining to 'the days of creation.' Lastly, a study of biblical words in their original Hebrew and Greek text sources gives us confidence in God's inerrant and beautifully and poetically written word to inspire and strengthen us spiritually while providing solid hope for the future.

We all know that the same words can mean quite different things to different people because of our individual differences in age, sex, place of birth, nationality, education and language. This chapter presents a linguistic, semantic understanding to the word "day" or "*yom*" in Hebrew as used in the Genesis creation account.

In the previous chapter we considered the beginning of God's six-creation days as found in Genesis 1 and 2. This chapter establishes the lengths of time involved in creation according to information contained in the Bible record, knowledge gleaned from historical geological observations, readings, as well as linguistic and semantic studies.

One sure way to reach a correct understanding for the length of the word *day* as found in Genesis 1 is semantics, the scientific analysis of words. This approach is a reliable path to understand the correct meaning for the length of days as given in God's six creation days where the Hebrew word *yom* is used. Most scientists agree that the intended meaning of words as established through semantic analysis is practically indisputable. Biblical interpretation cannot be left in the hands of unscientific speculators using the rationale of "I think it means," where everyone has an individual but unqualified opinion. To accept this kind of thinking is to tolerate the world of unbelief. Forming opinions through inconsistent personal reasoning is dangerously parallel to non-Bible studying Christians or non-believers professing, "You can make the Bible say anything you want it to." Such thinking puts us at risk of losing faith in the authority of God's written word throughout the entire Bible.

If Satan convinces us that Genesis 1-11 is a fable or folklore, we may begin to question all Holy Scriptures, even those presenting the death and resurrection of our Lord, as the very basis for salvation. For these reasons, using semantic analysis to understand the key elements of creation is essential in obtaining the wisdom and knowledge that God intended us to have from His Word.

The term "Ancient of Days" in Daniel 7 is an authoritative statement indicating that God exists before the beginning of time and helps determine the length of Creation's days. In 2 Peter 3:8, we read "with the Lord one day is like a thousand years, and a thousand years like one day." This metaphor indicates the timelessness of God in His patience towards mankind.

"Those were the days, my friend; we thought they'd never end..." According to *Wikipedia*, "this is a song credited to Gene Raskin, who put English lyrics to the Russian Gypsy song 'Dorogoi dlinnoyu'" These lyrics describe an era of joviality in the lifetime of humans when hearts were light and fancy free.

The Longest Day is the title of a World War II movie covering the invasion of Normandy, France, and describing the hardships and horrors experienced by the Allied military during one day that seemed to last forever.

The instruction, "Just take one day at a time..." is commonly heard in every Alcoholics Anonymous (AA) meeting, expressing the fact that a 24-hour day is all that our Creator God gives us and that we should live our very best during this day, and every day given thereafter.

There are countless additional usages and meanings for the word "day" as well as for other common phrases denoting time. The English language contains fourteen distinct definitions for the word "day" alone. Similarly, Hebrew language has five definitions for the word *yom*, or *yhom*, their usage for the word "day." All definitions for the Hebrew word *yom* follow:

    1) a period of light in a night/day cycle;

    2) *a period of 24-hours;

    3) a general or vague concept of time;

    4) a specific point of time;

    5) a period of a year.

*Item 2 is the proper definition found for the Hebrew word *yom* adopted in this analysis of Genesis 1 and 2 for the Creation period.

We can learn much from studying the Bible concerning its use of semantics. First of all, 2 Timothy 3:15 tells us that the Bible's purpose is to reveal God's message to mankind: "and that from childhood you have known the sacred writings which are able to give you the wisdom that leads to salvation through faith which is in Christ Jesus."

Secondly, as Christians we consider the Bible to be the inerrant, inspired word of God as stated in 2 Timothy 3:16, "All Scripture is inspired by God and profitable for teaching, for reproof, for correction, for training in righteousness;"

Using semantics in Bible study means analyzing the word meaning and groups of words taken in their intended contexts. The analysis of these word forms is used to arrive at the most logical understandable meaning of the author, God, as expressed through His writers. 2 Peter 1:20-21 says, [20]"But know this first of all, that no prophecy of Scripture is *a matter* of one's own interpretation, [21]for no prophecy was ever made by an act of human will, but men moved by the Holy Spirit spoke from God."

The interpretation of the length and meaning of the word

"day," or the Hebrew word *yom,* is semantically analyzed using other Old Testament writings. One particularly outstanding study is by semantics expert, James Stambaugh, in "The days of creation: A semantic approach." This well-respected semanticist establishes the length and duration of creation days by analyzing the Hebrew word *yom* (day) and in the process confirms scripture's inerrancy. To accomplish this task, I quote part of his semantic analysis of the Hebrew word *yom* (day):

> The word *yom* occurs 2,291 times in the Old Testament, appearing in the singular form 1,446 times and 845 times in the plural. However, only the singular form of *yom* appears in Genesis 1, which indicates a short period of time. But both singular and plural forms of *yom* occur frequently with a preposition. These differences are mentioned because they do affect the meaning of the word regarding length of time.
>
> The Old Testament writings where the word *yom* is found are the historical books, the poetic books and the prophetic books. To be as consistent as possible in interpreting the word *yom*, it first should be contextually analyzed within its genre in the historical books because the meaning can sometimes change slightly within the different genres of the Old Testament writings. However, nearly every difference in meaning appears obvious when word analysis is given within its context in each genre.

Stambaugh depends upon analysis of the word *yom* in Genesis 1 to arrive at God's intended meaning for the length of days in the six days of creation. All of his referencing and analysis for the word *yom* is taken outside of Genesis 1. Mr. Stambaugh demonstrates the proper method to arrive at the meaning of an unknown word is to compare it with the meanings of the same word whose meaning are known from their consistent use in other text portions. Although not totally exhaustive, this study should convince us without doubt as to the length of day God used in His creation process.

As seen in Stambaugh's findings, the meaning of *yom* when used in that form is interpreted and supported in the Old Testament by its association with other grammatical forms influencing its meaning. Associated terminologies found in Genesis 1 are first the numbers, and secondly the words *morning, evening, light, night,* and *darkness.*

There are two recognized classifications for the use of *yom* with numbers; these are the cardinal numbers (e.g. one, two, three, etc.), and ordinal numbers, (first, second... seventh, etc.). In the Genesis 1 account of creation's Day One, cardinal numbers are used. However, in the series for days *second* through *seventh,* ordinal numbers are used. I do not consider this a significant variation in understanding the meaning of *yom* as it also occurs in the series numbering the seven days of creation. Taken in context, the meaning is one day, whether or not the number is cardinal or ordinal. In the same article, Stambaugh also quotes semanticist Terence Fretheim as saying, "When the word 'day' is used with a specific number, it always has reference to a normal day." Fretheim also notes that when the word *yom* is observed with numbers occurring in succession in a specific context, it denotes a solar day.

Building on Stambaugh's findings, Newman is a theologian who declares that there are no clear examples of the use of *yom* with an ordinal number that indicate a long period of time. This confirms that when *yom* is combined with a number, the intended meaning is a 24-hour day.

Yom and numbers are also used to include a prepositional phrase. The use of *yom* and an ordinal number with the prepositions 'on' or 'for' adds to the meaning of a 24-hour day that an action has taken place. In every case presenting the six-day creation event, the phrase, "And there was evening and there was morning," is used to function in the manner of a preposition. In the following scriptures, this prepositional rule is underlined in its locational use.

In Exodus 24:16, "The glory of the LORD rested on Mount Sinai, and the cloud covered it for six days; and on the seventh day, He called to Moses from the midst of the cloud." In this passage the preposition *on* indicates an ongoing event throughout this seven-day period. Although Genesis 1 does not identically fit this mold, similarities are apparent. This same relationship supports the significance of a solar day associated with the use of *yom* and an ordinal number through the descriptive prepositional function of the words throughout Genesis 1, "There was evening and there was morning." This same wording is consistent in describing the second through the sixth days. This usage is similar to the prepositional use of *on* in Exodus 24 quoted above. Therefore, using numbers in association with *yom*, combined with the self-explanatory prepositional application of the phrase, "and there was evening and there was morning," indicates a 24-hour solar day for the action described.

Yom and numbers are used in a series in both Genesis 1 and in Numbers chapters 7 and 29. When *yom* is used with a number, it refers to a 24-hour day. Therefore, the question arises as to whether its use in a series indicates the 24-hour days are consecutive or if there could be gaps between the 24-hour days. While the latter is possible, it lacks credibility in the contextual use of items in a numbered series.

In both Genesis 1 and Numbers 7, the phrasing does not exactly define a consecutive sequence of days. However, in Numbers 29, the days are clearly defined as consecutive 24-hour days. Proper grammatical usage for items in a parallel series indicates equality unless modified with a qualifying remark such as "in that order." This would indicate the importance of the numerical order in that sequential line of parallel reasoning. There is no modifier in the sequential numbering of the days in Genesis 1 to indicate any change in the basic parallel rules of grammar. Neither is variance to this rule found in Numbers 7 and 29.

Each day in Creation's six days is worded the same internally with no indication that one day is any different than any other. No modifiers state differently. Therefore, we can conclude logically that all of the days were 24-hour periods occurring in seven consecutive days as revealed contextually. This matches the modern-day interpretation of our calendar week.

The use of *yom* with the combined words "morning" and "evening," either used with *yom* (19 times), or independently lacking the word *yom* (38 times), always indicates a 24-hour solar day regardless of whether the genre is a historical, poetic or prophetic Old Testament book.

When the word *night* is used in any of the three Old Testament genres with the word *yom*, it always indicates a solar day. This occurs 53 times.

The use of the words *light* and *darkness* may be used individually or in combination with each other. The word *light* appears with the word *yom* 15 times in all genres with slightly different but readily anticipated additional meanings. Twelve times it refers to the usual concept of the cycle of light and darkness implying a 24-hour solar day. On three other occasions it is used figuratively to declare God's power in a future time. Those three instances are all found in the prophetic genre.

Darkness is found in conjunction with *yom* 11 times in all three genres. In seven of these occurrences it is used figuratively.

In Ecclesiastes it is used once to indicate a coming time of trouble: "Indeed, if a man should live many years, let him rejoice in them all, and let him remember days of darkness, for they will be many. Everything that is to come *will be* futility." (Ecclesiastes 11:8)

The other six figurative uses are found in the prophetic genre indicating a future time when God will demonstrate His power to mankind as in Isaiah 29:18, "On that day the deaf will hear words of a book, and out of *their* gloom and darkness the eyes of the blind will see."

Out of the 26 times either "light" or "darkness" is used with *yom* in the Old Testament, it is only found four times in the historical narrative genre. In all four of those cases the referral is to time within mankind's commonly known experience of a 24-hour solar day. Other words used in Genesis 1 phrases in combination with *yom* further substantiate these findings when linked to numbers to again mean 24-hour solar days.

A summary analysis of *yom* study shows biblical proof of God's six 24-hour sequential days for the act of creating the heavens and the earth as Genesis records. In the following chapter, concluding evidence for 24-hour days will also be addressed concerning additional available words *not* used to describe day. Chapters 3 and 4 on linguistics and semantics should solidify our quest to establish the Bible's inerrancy and reliability, particularly as they pertain to Genesis 1-11 and the six-day creation account:

We are to take one day at a time,
From dawn to dawn we are guided sometimes,
His Holy Word is our delight,
When in the Bible we maintain our sight.

His word is inerrant, you'll see,
He guided us throughout history,
Guided in truth for all to perceive,
His love shines forth from His word received.

Chapter 4
LENGTH OF DAYS:
MORE LINGUISTICS AND SEMANTICS

*In that day I will raise up the fallen booth of David, and wall up its breaches;
I will also raise up its ruins and rebuild it as in the days of old.* AMOS 9:11

All of mankind is in need of salvation through knowledge of the truth. Through studying God's word, the Bible, we stand firm in the knowledge that Christ died for all. Examining and understanding semantics gives Bible readers confidence in the inerrant accuracy of the Holy Scripture. Often people can more readily understand what is meant by what is *not* said or written than by what *is* said or written. Consider words *not* used in the creation account that were available at the time of its writing. Semantic examination around the meaning of the word "day" in Genesis 1 is not complete until arguments against it are also considered, logically analyzed and refuted. These are arguments raised by opponents who simply state, "I think it means," while ignoring the facts gained through sound semantic analysis. This next section semantically analyzes other available Hebrew words which could have been used by God if His intention were to describe anything other than 24-hour days in the six-day Genesis creation account.

The plural use of *yom* indicates a long period of time. This is important to understand through semantic analysis to prove that the intent of the Bible's phrasing is extended only to times of historical significance to mankind. The extension of that Old Testament terminology to include billions of years, as "old earth theorists" imply, is semantically impossible. Instead, the plural form of *yom* is understood to indicate a set length of historical time dictated by the context in which it is used. Examples of this are found in the life of Bible personages, such as, "in the days of Moses," indicating past years of time when patriarchs walked the earth. However, two Hebrew words used in conjunction with the plural use of *yom* indicate lengthy time spans of thousands of years. These words are translated respectively as "of old" and "eternal." In both cases these words translate within their contexts to indicate a period of time "of old."

The word "eternal" in Hebrew can be viewed in Amos 9:11, "In that day I will raise up the fallen booth of David, and wall up its breaches; I will also raise up its ruins and rebuild it as in the days of old;" Here the word is translated as "days of old" because of its referral to the time of the destruction of Jerusalem in predicting the rebuilding of that same city back to its original condition. This meaning applies to a known period of history and is therefore not translated *eternal* as in the *eternal existence of God*. Although "Old earth" theorists may try to apply it as meaning millions and billions of years, they can be refuted by the historical context provided within the prophetical genre where this word is found. Plural usage for *yom*, which would have indicated more than one day, was not used in Genesis 1. Though available to the author of Genesis, this usage was not applied. Therefore, as determined by previous findings, it is assumed that only 24-hour days are indicated.

Another available time word indicating a short period of time includes *Rega,* translated as "instantly" or "moment" in Hebrew. See Exodus 33:5, "For the LORD had said to Moses, 'Say to the sons of Israel, you are an obstinate people; should I go up in your midst for <u>one moment</u>, I would destroy you. Now therefore, put off your ornaments from you, that I may know what I shall do with you.'"

It is significant that this word is not used in the interpretation of the meaning of *day.* The meaning of day in the creation account cannot be misconstrued to mean "instantly" as in the New Testament interpretation of the time of the coming of our Lord as in the statement, "We will be changed in the twinkling of an eye." Therefore, God did not create everything instantly, but in consecutive 24-hour increments as previously established by referencing Stambaugh's article. The following time words indicate long periods of time:

> e*t* - indicates "time" in general
> *ad* - the word "forever" when used with a preposition
> *qedem* - sometimes translated "as old"
> *nesah* - denotes "always" or "forever"
> *tamid* - means "continually" or "forever"

olam - translated "perpetual," "of old" or "forever"

dor - signifies "generation"

orek - translated as "length of days"when used with "*yom*"

zeman - denotes a "season" or "time"

moed - also "season"

yamim - plural days

Although available to the author, no Hebrew words indicating long periods of time were used in the Genesis 1 account indicating the length of each day. Therefore, the conclusion seems obvious that since these words were available to indicate age-old creation periods, they would have been chosen by our loving God for clear documentation regarding Moses, if necessary. For that reason, proof for the 24-hour day remains valid.

In addition, there are four ways in Hebrew to indicate ongoing creation time beginning in the past but continuing on into the future that were not used in Genesis 1:

1) *olam,* "perpetual" modified by the preposition *le* used with "days" or "morning and evening." If this use were implemented, it could be interpreted as an ongoing creation event initiated in the past and continuing on into the future commonly believed by theistic evolutionists.

2) *dor,* "generation" used alone or in combination with "days," "days and nights" or "morning and evening" could have indicated, "generations of days and nights."

3) *tamid,* "continual" used with "days," "days and nights," or "morning and evening" could have been translated to mean, "a continuation of days."

4) ad, "forever" used by itself or with the conjunction *olam* could be used to indicate a summary statement of, "and it was forever."

The fact that this terminology was not used also indicates that the intent was to indicate 24-hour days in the creation event rather than longer periods of time. The significance of this is that the belief system of theistic evolutionists is discredited. Theistic evolutionists believe that God created everything ages ago and that all of creation has been evolving ever since, without God's help. Analyzing grammatical order and construction helps readers recognize and refute attempts to lure them into unreliable belief systems.

It is evident that if God desired to communicate an ongoing and evolutionary creation process, the above four applications of the Hebrew language could have been applied to achieve that meaning. However, that is not the case. Therefore, again, our previous proof for a 24-hour solar day remains valid.

Yom is used singularly with a number to indicate an "era" as in Zechariah 14:1-11. There are always some people that want to believe in evolution and a godless creation that try to refute the surmounting data of semantic evidence for 24-hour long days during the creation event. One disputed source is found in Zechariah 14:7, "For it will be a unique day which is known to the LORD, neither day nor night, but it will come about that at evening time there will be light." This verse is a prophetic genre with obvious figurative meaning. It is great exaggeration to try to apply this example of *yom* with a number ("a" indicating one) as applicable to the intent of the length of a day in Genesis 1, or indeed, anywhere in the Bible where a 24-hour day is indicated. As in real estate where "location, location, location" is totally important in the evaluation of property, so "genre and context, genre and context, genre and context" are equally vitally important in using semantics to evaluate meaning.

Other rebuttals to a 24-hour day in Genesis 1 include the use of "day" in Genesis 2:4 to refute the 24-hour day rule for the six days of creation. Consider the verse, "This is the account of the heavens and the earth when they were created, in the day that the LORD God made earth and heaven." This was discussed earlier as being common usage in Hebrew literature, as it is in English, indicating a time period such as, "in my father's day." This rebuttal is easily refuted by context and obvious intent. Other reasons this passage does not work as an argument for creationist opponents is the lack of the use of either a number or the words in Genesis 1 of "night," "light and darkness," "morning and evening," all supportive of 24-hour days. This additional terminology is lacking in Genesis 2:4. Instead, the usage of the word "day" logically and textually indicates the "days of creation" or "the week of creation."

Another issue to contend with is the argument that solar days could not be meant because the sun, moon and stars were not created until Day Four. On Day One of creation, God created light and darkness. A 24-hour day is not necessarily dependent on the shining of the sun as we know it to create a solar day. A 24-hour period occurs with a single rotation of our earth. A source of light emanates at God's will, even from Himself, as described throughout the Bible as one of God's identifying qualities. All that is needed for the events of creation prior to Day Four is a source of light to make a difference between "light and darkness," "evening and morning."

This list of alternative examples is by no means exhaustive but is included to show you that arguments occur to attempt to compromise peoples' belief in the inerrancy of scripture. Consider this a wakeup call and beware of the onslaught of unbelief that targets the faith and beliefs of Christians.

It is important not to accept unfounded arguments against a 24-hour solar day as shown in Genesis 1. If we accept such arguments put forward by non-believers that Genesis 1 is uniquely a "God day," not occurring elsewhere anywhere in scripture or in other Hebrew writings, and not a specific literal 24-hour solar day as indicated by semantics, we open the door to questioning any and all wording in the Bible. However, careful semantic analysis of the Bible's wording reveals no available proofs to support such findings. Opinions differing from the stated analyzed Word of God are personal conjecture without historical or scientific proof. No one was there during creation to record the event, outside of the Father, Son and Holy Spirit, and possibly some form of angelic beings. The inspired account, recorded in scripture, is the only true record supported by current scientific and archaeological discoveries. If we challenge the meaning of the semantic use of words there as irrelevant, we enter fruitless realms of philosophical reasoning where nothing we write or say means what we intend it to write or say. This becomes circuitous reasoning too nonsensical to comprehend.

Undoubtedly, additional arguments are lodged by opponents to the young earth theory in an attempt to refute the 24-hour days of Genesis 1. However, Christian theologians and scientists have disproved many godless theories with adequate proofs for centuries. Though godless theorists occasionally admit that they *may have been wrong* in some instances, they seldom say, "Now I see—now I finally believe there is a holy, righteous God." Romans 1:18–20 states: [18]"For the wrath of God is revealed from heaven against all ungodliness and unrighteousness of men who suppress the truth in unrighteousness, [19]because that which is known about God is evident within them; for God made it evident to them. [20]For since the creation of the world His invisible attributes, His eternal power and divine nature, have been clearly seen, being understood through what has been made, so that they are without excuse."

Not everyone that is not a creationist who has another belief system is necessarily an enemy of God. The fact that some people don't understand the Bible's truth may be because they haven't had it clearly presented. Our role is to proclaim and explain God's truth without antagonism whenever and wherever possible. When we do so we usually have no way of knowing whether our words are being heard and received or rejected. Proverbs 19:25 says, "Strike a scoffer and the naive may become shrewd, but reprove one who has understanding and he will gain knowledge."

Belief is supremely important in the lives of mature Christians. We do not have to struggle with others who refuse belief in scripture's inerrancy. What is important is that we confidently believe God's written word. In so doing we gain greater confidence in God, confidence in ourselves before God, confidence before the people of the world, and become an encouragement to all in the family of God who do believe. This results in greater faith in and knowledge of the rock of our salvation, Jesus Christ.

Stand firm in your belief in the Bible's inerrancy. Many may attempt to compromise our belief in scripture hoping to shake our belief in God and salvation through His Son. Many cults claim to have answers on everything written in the Bible and twist scriptures to bring deception. They often create illusions in an effort to allure believers away from the family of God, professing to be truthful while really misguiding hearers into slavery. In a televised news interview many years ago, even Billy Graham openly admitted that there are many mysteries in the Bible that he does not yet understand. Although there are many things in the Bible we may never fully understand, this does not leave us lacking in knowledge and wisdom.

As one theologian stated, "I didn't write the Bible. I don't have to defend it." Although all people we encounter need the wisdom and knowledge God provides through studying His word, in most cases where the enemy raises conflicts to compromise belief, it is best just to walk away when possible. We can usually tell the difference between an enemy attack and a genuinely inquisitive mind. Don't be afraid to present godly wisdom for the seeker's salvation may be at stake. The Bible tells us to be as wise as a serpent and as harmless as a dove. Beware and take care, but don't be afraid to express the reason for the hope that we have within us as Colossians 2:8–10 says, [8]"See to it that no one takes you captive through philosophy and empty deception, according to the tradition of men, according to the elementary principles of the world, rather than according to Christ. [9]For in Him all the fullness of Deity dwells in bodily form, [10]and in Him you have been made complete, and He is the head over all rule and authority;"

This provides the preliminary information needed to remove many boulders in faith's roadway in order to pave the way for the most spectacular seven days in the history of the world, the creation of everything that we see around us. One day we will perfectly understand this wonderful creation of our Holy God and properly steward it for our benefit and God's glory.

A day is measured from time to time,
With the thoughts of eternity in mind.
The mind of man can oft perceive,
Time extended beyond belief.

A day to one is measured from sun to sun,
This is contradicted by another one.
A day as seen by one man's eye,
Must be stated clearly or be denied.

SEVEN DAYS AND BEYOND
Chapters 5-12

Chapter 5

THE SEVEN DAYS OF CREATION: LIGHT - DAY ONE

And there will no longer be any night; and they will not have need of the light of a lamp nor the light of the sun, because the Lord God will illumine them; and they will reign forever and ever. REVELATION 22:5

Light emanated from a special source from God on Creation's Day One. This light source was prior to and independent of the stars and other planetary bodies in the universe which God had not yet created. Light described in the Bible is not only physical, but also spiritual and moral, emanating from the heart of truth. In the Book of John, Jesus is described as being the light of the world, as are we, when we follow Him. The Bible contrasts light and darkness, with light being the reward for the godly and darkness being reserved for the ungodly. The dark recess of a godless existence is not the place any of us want to go. Instead, living in the light of Christ and enjoying and abiding with Him in God's kingdom is the hope of every believer.

In spite of our diligence, we yet have human limitations in Bible understanding. For any analysis of the written Bible, we must acknowledge the miraculous powers of our Creator and Lord as exhibited through the actions of the Holy Trinity. The Bible tells us how to live our lives successfully and in ways pleasing to our Maker. It does not give us detailed action plans for how to proceed or follow for every occurrence we encounter in our lifetimes. However, it does give us enough information to understand and take the proper action when encountering unexpected trials.

There are many mysteries in the Bible known only to our Creator. As His people, we can only conjecture about some of God's actions concerning What? Why? How? All of these questions have been asked by the prophets of old as well as by theologians today. There are things stated in the Bible that we must accept on faith that are not explainable through any present sources. I personally believe that God honors our curiosity and even our misdirected and feeble attempts to discover how and why He has established some of this world's social and natural laws. His creation process is just one of the miraculous acts God has not yet explained to us in detail. However, there are enough written clues in the Bible through progressive revelation to enable us to arrive at a reasonable hypothesis for its sequences and occurrences, and hence for the probable development of the creation process seen on earth today and in the natural record.

Some God-fearing scientists have made inroads into these mysterious acts of God with some success in discovering and applying these laws to the benefit of mankind. Other scientifically-motivated investigators have also made discoveries and suppositions with mixed results. Some of their natural and social logic and sequential reasoning is very good, but at times limited due to not incorporating God's wisdom. This failure to incorporate God into their theorization results in a skewed and frequently distorted misapplication of God's laws which becomes of questionable value to mankind. However, the research completed by Christian and non-Christian scientists in the social and natural sciences benefits both mankind and our theological knowledge when this information is gathered without bias in an attempt to arrive at the truth.

The following information concerning the six days of creation, as well as the seventh day of rest, is my attempt to apply my studies of science and theology in as unbiased a way as my heart and mind can accomplish. This information is gained from my background in natural resources along with my theology study through both formal and informal education supplemented by my best analysis of the available information. Of course, none of us were there during these six days of creation. The only persons present were the Father, Son and Holy Spirit along with possibly others of the heavenly host of angelic beings. Information of this miraculous act is limited only by inspiration of God to those recording this data in the Holy Scripture, the Bible; 2 Timothy 3:16 says, "All Scripture is inspired by God and profitable for teaching, for reproof, for correction, for training in righteousness;"

Preview of Creation's Seven Days—As described in the Bible's opening verses in Genesis 1:1-2, God's first creation was matter: "In the beginning God created the heavens and the earth. ²The earth was formless and void, and darkness was over the surface of the deep…" The terms formless and void indicate a lack of life and structure. "The deep" seems to indicate formless matter throughout space in a fluid universe. "and the Spirit of God was moving over the surface of the waters." The Holy Spirit of God hovered over this mass of water in the creation process of the heavens and earth. In 2 Peter 3:5, the Apostle Peter describes this formation: "For when they maintain this, it escapes their notice that by the word of God *the* heavens existed long ago and *the* earth was formed out of water and by water." From this correlation we can assume that in the pre-creation universe, matter was in a liquid state with all elements common to our earth, and probably the universe, carried in suspension.

Day One, "Let There Be Light"

Notice that God's creation of light and then separating it from darkness receives emphasis in the Bible's opening verses. Genesis 1:3-4: ³"Then God said, 'Let there be light'; and there was light. ⁴God saw that the light was good; and God separated the light from the darkness…" This light may well have been light emanating from God himself, seeing that the luminous heavenly bodies, the sun, moon and stars, were not created until the Day Four. Therefore, the light created throughout the universe must specifically have been located in God as to source of origin. The two opposites, light and darkness, seemingly exist simultaneously in this description. In the creation process, as most of us understand it, God creates a shadow of darkness from an outside light source due to the reference to day and night given in Genesis 1:5. On Creation's Day One, light was created. Again, the phrase light and darkness is used in Genesis 1:14 on Creation's Day Four when the sun, moon and stars were created as luminaries.

Because God Himself is widespread visible light, Revelation 22:5 tells us that we will have no need of the sun, moon and other luminaries in God's new eternal day: "And there will no longer be *any* night; and they will not have need of the light of a lamp nor the light of the sun, because the Lord God will illumine them; and they will reign forever and ever." In this scripture, light appears to emanate from God Himself, invading every nook and cranny of the universe. Further substantiation of God's light is given in Revelation 21:23-24 with the arrival of the new heavenly Jerusalem: [23]"And the city has no need of the sun or of the moon to shine on it, for the glory of God has illumined it, and its lamp *is* the Lamb. [24]The nations will walk by its light, and the kings of the earth will bring their glory into it." In this passage the light source is described as a lamp who is Christ, the Lamb of God. This also refers to the city, the New Jerusalem. However, the light of Christ appears greatest of all, indicating it will be a light for the nations as well.

The following scriptures show God establishing a limited, visible, or invisible light source seemingly apparent to only a few. A fascinating occurrence of this happens to all of Egypt prior to Israel's Exodus journey when one of the plagues envelopes everything in total darkness except for the homes of the Israelites. See Exodus 10:22-23: [22]"So Moses stretched out his hand toward the sky, and there was thick darkness in all the land of Egypt for three days. [23]They did not see one another, nor did anyone rise from his place for three days, but all the sons of Israel had light in their dwellings."

Another case of unexplainable but observable light was experienced by Saul in Acts 9:3 while he was on the road to Damascus pursuing Christians to persecute: "As he (Paul) was traveling, it happened that he was approaching Damascus, and suddenly a light from heaven flashed around him;" These scriptures establish that God Himself is able to provide a source of light aside from literal physical suns, moons and stars placed wonderfully throughout the universe.

In addition, I'm aware of numerous recent reports of light occurring in home churches throughout Communist China but not resulting from any power source known to man. These unsanctioned Chinese home churches require black-out conditions at night to avoid detection by (and persecution from) watchful communists. However, God often furnishes these believers with light, enabling them to read and worship in darkness. This information is frequently given on Christian radio, television, or in printed matter. Much of it is considered common knowledge in Christian circles. Frequent ethereal lightings in China are just some of the little advertised happenings accompanying the gaining of non-believers to Christ throughout Asia and the Middle-East.

In Genesis 1:5, "God called the light day, and the darkness He called night. And there was evening and there was morning, one day." God created light and darkness. Revelation 21 indicates that in God's city the Lamb is the lamp or light source where people from all nations will walk in and out of His light. It is also apparent that God can create light whenever and wherever He pleases, and to any magnitude He desires. To establish the light and darkness in the description of evening and morning indicates a point of light source creating day and night with respective light and shadow. This source of light could be within the pre-existent solar system or somewhere in infinite space. This is apparently what our Creator has done in order to say, "one day," with the implication of a 24-hour solar day.

To establish a 24-hour solar day, as scripture implies, requires some rotation of the pre-formed watery earth, which at that time was without form. "Without form and void" *may* mean devoid of life and without specific mass. The phrase, "The Spirit of God moved over the surface of the deep" indicates something pre-formed, but not yet sculpted. On Day Two of creation, the implication is that there was perhaps a blob of water out in space, and perhaps many such blobs throughout the universe, prior to God's separation of the sky and sea. All that is necessary to create a solar day is for the water mass to turn and churn to create the sequence of day and night with an outside light source who was almost certainly God in Christ, God's eternally-present Son.

One last item concerning light and darkness is God placing His light in the hearts and lives of believers outside of God's physical universe, while reserving places of darkness for Satan and his fallen angels. This probably also includes that part of humanity who refuse to be redeemed by God's grace.

As we read and analyze the Bible's declarations, on the first day of creation, literal and figurative places of darkness existed throughout the universe. These references include fallen, satanic angels, but also those humans who have fallen under deceitful influence and refuse belief in the redemption provided through Jesus, the Son of God. Consider these verses concerning the darkness reserved for fallen angels: 2 Peter 2:4, "For if God did not spare angels when they sinned, but cast them into hell and committed them to pits of darkness, reserved for judgment;" Also Jude 1:6, "And angels who did not keep their own domain, but abandoned their proper abode, He has kept in eternal bonds under darkness for the judgment of the great day,"

Other verses expounding on the darkness appointed for fallen mankind include Jude 1:10, "But these men revile the things which they do not understand; and the things which they know by instinct, like unreasoning animals, by these things they are destroyed." Consider also Jude 1:13, "wild waves of the sea, casting up their own shame like foam; wandering stars, for whom the black darkness has been reserved forever." 2 Peter 2:17 adds, "These are springs without water and mists driven by a storm, for whom the black darkness has been reserved." Rather than merely promising destruction, the Bible gives these and other graphic, tragic scriptures to warn us of things to come. God is merciful, desiring all of mankind to come to repentance and receive His salvation provided for all. The Bible says that everything written in it is for our benefit so that we do not make the same mistakes that early Israel did in their journey (see I Corinthians 10:1-13, as well as many references throughout the entire Book of Hebrews). Over and over in scripture, God instructs early Israel reasonably as a loving father would his son. In fact, the entire chapter of Deuteronomy 28 is one such lengthy passage providing clear instruction on the importance of our human choice. Major blessings result when God's people walk in obedience to God versus encountering the curses and destruction earned when departing from His ways.

Today we can personally know and experience God forgiving and forgetting all sins and shortcomings when we turn to Him and forsake our errant ways. In Micah 7:19, God marvelously speaks of burying our sins forever in the deep sea of His forgetfulness. Psalm 103:11-12 tells of putting them as far away from Himself as the east is from the west. Wonderfully, the doom and destruction of eternal darkness can be avoided. All who personally accept and believe in the name and life of Jesus and in His finished work on the cross can look forward to the promise of enjoying glorious life throughout eternity with Him.

2 Corinthians 4:6 says, "For God, who said, 'Light shall shine out of darkness,' is the One who has shone in our hearts to give the Light of the knowledge of the glory of God in the face of Christ." The significance of the creation of light, here metaphorically in believers' hearts, refers to Christ and His body of believers. In John 8:12, "Then Jesus again spoke to them, saying, 'I am the Light of the world; he who follows Me will not walk in the darkness, but will have the Light of life.'" Matthew 5:16 states, "Let your light shine before men in such a way that they may see your good works, and glorify your Father who is in heaven." In these cases, Christ is the light. However, Christ acknowledges that we, as believers and followers of Him and His teachings, are also the purveyors of His light that illuminates the hearts and minds of mankind.

Scripture urges us to pray that all of humanity receives redemption's salvation and escapes the horrors of eternal separation from God. Make application of these truths and follow God's instructions in verses like 2 Peter 3:9, "The Lord is not slow about His promise, as some count slowness, but is patient toward you, not wishing for any to perish but for all to come to repentance." Also read Titus 2:11-13 [11]"For the grace of God has appeared, bringing salvation to all men, [12]instructing us to deny ungodliness and worldly desires and to live sensibly, righteously and godly in the present age, [13]looking for the blessed hope and the appearing of the glory of our great God and Savior, Christ Jesus, to God in Christ is our hope and salvation. Though the earth be removed; yet will I put my hope in our Creator, the God of our salvation the Creator of all darkness and light." Finally, 1 Peter 2:9-10 describes God calling us out of the darkness: "Therefore, let us encourage one another daily to walk forward together in His marvelous light:"

Light must emanate from time to time,
From within this heart of mine.
This at times is hard to fathom,
Due to sin's created chasm.

Christ has come to all mankind,
Creating light to the end of time,
Shining within and without our lives,
This world's dreads are put to flight.

Chapter 6
SEPARATION OF THE WATERS: DAY TWO

The LORD by wisdom founded the earth, by understanding He established the heavens. by His knowledge the deeps were broken up and the skies drip with dew. PROVERBS 3:19-20

By God's wisdom and understanding, the firmament was separated from the seas. The Genesis account is substantiated by poetic utterances throughout the Bible ascribing wisdom in heavenly references not only to the physical creation, but also regarding the light and revelation given to mankind. To God belongs all of the honor, praise and glory for what He has done through His Son.

Genesis 1:6-8 expresses, ⁶"Then God said, 'Let there be an expanse in the midst of the waters, and let it separate the waters from the waters.' ⁷God made the expanse, and separated the waters which were below the expanse from the waters which were above the expanse; and it was so. ⁸God called the expanse heaven. And there was evening and there was morning, a second day."

On Creation's Day Two, the waters of earth were separated from the expanse above the earth, creating sky and seas. Many places in scripture, *heaven* is used interchangeably with *sky,* along with additional connotations relating to the stars of the universe and to the place where God dwells. Genesis 1:6-8 deals with the sky as it was known at that time, although it may have appeared quite differently then than today. At that early point, apparently evaporation and condensation from the previously described *element soup* created a cloud canopy. This separation then left *element soup* in the seas but with the distillation of pure water in the sky, more as we know it today, but perhaps with adaptations.

Just how God separated the waters from the waters is not fully understood today. Airline pilots speak of the height of the *ceiling,* which at the same time is the *base* of cloud formations. Such formations may extend upwards of 80,000 feet or close to sixteen miles of elevation to the near fringes of earth's outer atmosphere. Also today's weather forecasters may call a storm system *a cell,* though in reality it may be many separate *cells* making up a whole.

Such terminology parallels that used to describe mountains and mountain ranges. Alaska's Mt McKinley is made up of small mountains considered to be part of the large total mountain of that name. At the same time McKinley is part of the larger Alaska Range. The Bible does not offer detailed information on the separation process resulting in sky and sea, but does provide more than we know apart from the Bible's explanation.

Interesting data is available in articles by several expert NASA meteorologists who comment on aspects of condensation and the formation of rain, snow and hail. However, it is still hard to differentiate between individual clouds in homogenous units existing separately from other cloud bodies in the atmosphere.

Job 26:8 says, "He wraps up the waters in His clouds, and the cloud does not burst under them." That verse appears to relate cloud formation to the properties of water, condensation particles, electrical properties and individual temperature and atmospheric pressure gradients all contributing to the individuality of cloud cells. To date these factors have not been discussed with satisfactory scientific treatise regarding the distinctive homogeneity between individual clouds and cloud bodies. However, as shown, the Bible does describe these things in detail.

Jesus Christ as one-third of the Godhead was fully involved in the creation of the sky, seas, and of all that was made. John 1 describes Him as the "Word," and Proverbs 8 as "wisdom and understanding." The "Living Word" and His creative involvement have been discussed in earlier chapters. Wisdom and understanding being powerfully present in the creative process will be discussed next.

Proverbs 8:27-30 declares, [27]"When He established the heavens, I was there, when He inscribed a circle on the face of the deep, [28]when He made firm the skies above, when the springs of the deep became fixed, [29]when He set for the sea its boundary so that the water would not transgress His command, when He marked out the foundations of the earth; [30]then I was beside Him, *as* a master workman; and I was daily *His* delight, rejoicing always before Him." Proverbs 3:19-20 adds, "The LORD by wisdom founded the earth, by understanding He established the heavens. By His knowledge the deeps were broken up and the skies drip with dew." Jeremiah 51:15-16 offers a glimpse into divine engineering: "It is He who made the earth by His power, who established the world by His wisdom, and by His understanding He stretched out the heavens. [16]When He utters His voice, *there is* a tumult of waters in the heavens, and He causes the clouds to ascend from the end of the earth; He makes lightning for the rain and brings forth the wind from His storehouses."

The powerful tumult of waters described here seems to indicate a huge disturbance within the boundaries of our earth during the separation of the waters into seas and sky. Job 28:24-28 provides more information: [24]"For He looks to the ends of the earth and sees everything under the heavens. [25]When He imparted weight to the wind and meted out the waters by measure, [26]When He set a limit for the rain and a course for the thunderbolt, [27]then He saw it and declared it; He established it and also searched it out. [28]And to man He said, 'Behold, the fear of the Lord, that is wisdom; And to depart from evil is understanding.'" This had to be a tremendous engineering accomplishment involving a supreme degree of mathematics and physics ability beyond our ability to speculate. God accomplished His creation measured out and governed precisely by His natural laws established throughout this world, and probably throughout the universe.

God's means of accomplishing such great feats is described in Psalms 33:6-7, "'By the word of the LORD the heavens were made, and by the breath of His mouth all their host. [7]He gathers the waters of the sea together as a heap; He lays up the deeps in storehouses." The phrase *gathering of the waters in a heap* also indicates a gargantuan disturbance throughout the earth. The *storehouses* mentioned may be something in reserve beyond the sight or comprehension of our human senses, and may in fact be beyond the boundaries of this earth's influence as currently known and understood by human limitations. Storehouses probably existed in pre-flood times within earth's bounds and were released at the time of the flood to cover the earth.

Indications of a different world than the one we presently know are expressed in Job 37:16-22 as God says, [16]"Do you know about the layers of the thick clouds, the wonders of one perfect in knowledge, [17]you whose garments are hot, when the land is still because of the south wind? [18]Can you, with Him, spread out the skies, strong as a molten mirror... [21]Now men do not see the light which is bright in the skies; but the wind has passed and cleared them. [22]Out of the north comes golden *splendor;* around God is awesome majesty.'"

This beautiful allegorical passage implies that the *strength of the skies* may have been stronger then than we observe today. Due to the vast amounts of fossil fuel deposits within our world in ancient times, we do understand that earlier climate patterns differed greatly from ours today.

The implications of an awesome God also are visible in the second day of Creation. But just who is this God made visible through His creation within His glorious seas and skies? The poetic books of Psalms, Proverbs and Job, along with the prophetic writings in Isaiah, all attest to the

Creator as the God of nature, wisdom, righteousness and understanding. These factors culminate in God sending His Son, Jesus, to accomplish our personal salvation and the redemption of this world we live in.

Psalms 77:13-18 states, [13]"Your way, O God, is holy; What God is great like our God?

[14]You are the God who works wonders; You have made known Your strength among the peoples. [15]You have by Your power redeemed Your people, The sons of Jacob and Joseph. *Selah.* [16]The waters saw You, O God; the waters saw You, they were in anguish; the deeps also trembled. [17]The clouds poured out water; the skies gave forth a sound; Your arrows flashed here and there. [18]The sound of Your thunder was in the whirlwind; the lightnings lit up the world; the earth trembled and shook."

From the very beginning, long before creation and before the written Bible introduces the patriarchs, our powerful Trinitarian Creator God made up of the three entities, Father, Son and Holy Spirit, has ruled over His people and all nature through the balanced order He set into motion and through which He operates. All praise, reverence, and honor is due to Him. Job 38:33-37 says, [33]"Do you know the ordinances of the heavens, or fix their rule over the earth? [34]Can you lift up your voice to the clouds, So that an abundance of water will cover you? [35]Can you send forth lightnings that they may go and say to you, 'Here we are'? [36]Who has put wisdom in the innermost being or given understanding to the mind? [37]Who can count the clouds by wisdom, or tip the water jars of the heavens,"

God's words to Job from the whirlwind show man's inability to comprehend higher ultimate things. Specifically, these verses highlight the awesome honor, respect and great dignity due Him from even our limited understanding of earlier verses plus Job 28:24-27 regarding God's amazing engineering feats in creating the skies and seas. God continues to speak through the clouds in Job 28:28 with a message inspiring even greater knowledge of and respect for the Creator: "And to man He said, 'Behold, the fear of the Lord, that is wisdom; and to depart from evil is understanding.'" From the clouds God speaks to His creation to aid our spiritual well-being and understanding. He is holy and righteous, deserving our attention to hear and obey His message to turn from evil. Then and only then can God give us the spiritual wisdom and insight we need to understand more of His character to interact more meaningfully with Him within His creation.

Isaiah 45:8 also declares God's righteousness from the heavens: [8]"'Drip down, O heavens, from above, and let the clouds pour down righteousness; let the earth open up and salvation bear fruit, and righteousness spring up with it. I, the LORD, have created it.'" It is the will of God that we become more like Him in all aspects of morality, integrity and righteousness. For this reason God sent His Son, Jesus, to earth that through His redemptive gift, provided through His death, resurrection and ascension two thousand years ago, we may live a redeemed life in forgiveness, wholeness, and righteousness.

Proverbs 3:19-26 adds that we should seek wisdom and the knowledge of God: [19]"'The LORD by wisdom founded the earth, by understanding He established the heavens. [20]By His knowledge the deeps were broken up and the skies drip with dew. ²¹My son, let them not vanish from your sight; Keep sound wisdom and discretion, ²²So they will be life to your soul and adornment to your neck. ²³Then you will walk in your way securely and your foot will not stumble. ²⁴When you lie down, you will not be afraid; when you lie down, your sleep will be sweet. ²⁵Do not be afraid of sudden fear nor of the onslaught of the wicked when it comes; ²⁶for the LORD will be your confidence and will keep your foot from being caught.'" The great benefits gained through our obedience are incomparably greater than "we can ask or think," both now and forevermore.

Jesus, the Word, Wisdom, Understanding—these and many other wonderful scripture names and terms are also used in analysis of the verses describing Creation's Day Two and indicate that all life is centered in the Word of God. If we hope to grow in His limitless eternal life, we should delight in feeding on His word, regularly learning and growing in wisdom and knowledge of Him. God never promised us an easy life. We have to accept the daily challenges and tests He permits which actually make us strong. He transforms hardships for our sakes to do us good, even when they may be the harvest of what we have earned through errant living. All humans naturally inherit trials and tribulations. Sometimes they are God-permitted reproofs to correct us where we or our ancestors have gone astray or been unwise and disobedient. Similar to the story of Job, God sometimes allows hardship to show us that He alone is faithful, sovereign, and in control of all things—to Him alone belongs the glory.

Psalms 19:1 tells us, "The heavens are telling of the glory of God; and their expanse is declaring the work of

His hands." This scripture points us to our creator, as do the natural visible glories of the land and skies of God's kingdom here on earth. Life and salvation are His hands through the person of the Son, Jesus Christ. As many scripture passages express, all nature declares the glory of God. The Bible tells us of the qualities of God and his grace through the Son. Study to learn and grow in God's grace daily. To Him belongs all the glory, honor and praise, forever. Amen.

The skies above the sea below,
Created by God in this earth we know,
His heavens require our awesome attention,
Their splendor exhibited beyond comprehension.

The seas as exhibited from times of old,
Instill power and strength to brave hearts untold.
The skies above the seas below,
Exhibit God's majesty to all whom He knows.

Chapter 7

LAND, SEAS AND VEGETATION: DAY THREE

From everlasting I was established, From the beginning, from the earliest times of the earth. When there were no depths I was brought forth, when there were no springs abounding with water. Before the mountains were settled, before the hills I was brought forth; While He had not yet made the earth and the fields, Nor the first dust of the world. PROVERBS 8:23-26

The land mass began solidifying in our globe as it separated from the liquid elements held in suspension in our newly forming world. Vegetation spread across the newly formed land mass within a hot-house like atmosphere of dense, steamy mist. All creation proceeded on schedule guided by the ever-loving hand of God in preparation for the appearance of man, the crown of His creation, three days hence.

Genesis 1:9-13 says, [9]"Then God said, 'Let the waters below the heavens be gathered into one place, and let the dry land appear'; and it was so. [10]God called the dry land earth, and the gathering of the waters He called seas; and God saw that it was good. [11]Then God said, 'Let the earth sprout vegetation: plants yielding seed, *and* fruit trees on the earth bearing fruit after their kind with seed in them'; and it was so. [12]The earth brought forth vegetation, plants yielding seed after their kind, and trees bearing fruit with seed in them, after their kind; and God saw that it was good. [13]There was evening and there was morning, a third day."

A friend of mine once stated that when it comes to the events of creation, scientists must say, "I don't know," but theologians must also say, "I don't know." The fact remains that no human was present, only the Father, Son and Holy Spirit—and perhaps some of God's created angelic beings. For this reason concerning all details of creation's formation, most of us must also say, "I don't know"—except for what the inspired word of God reveals to us as enhanced through the mind of Christ. Nor is much said in the Bible concerning mountain building except to state that it was done by God along with creation of all hills and valleys. The Bible's purpose is not to instruct us in the scientific realm of God's creation processes, but to make us wise unto salvation. In 2 Timothy 3:15 we read, "and that from childhood you have known the sacred writings which are able to give you the wisdom that leads to salvation through faith which is in Christ Jesus." Therefore much of this writing is evangelical in nature but accompanied by physical explanations derived from scientific evidence gathered from articles by Christian and secular scientists in their professional fields of expertise.

Concerning the gathering of the seas and the formation

of land masses, Genesis 1:9-10 tells us: [9]"Then God said, 'Let the waters below the heavens be gathered into one place, and let the dry land appear'; and it was so. [10]God called the dry land earth, and the gathering of the waters He called seas; and God saw that it was good."

We considered earlier that the pre-created morass of earth consisted of water best described as *element soup*. According to my understanding of physics and chemistry, this element soup was a mixture of super-saturated chemicals in a grand-style element bouilli (often pronounced *booya*). It only needed the finger of God to precipitate it into what we know today as water, rock, or soil with the added development of vegetation to cover the earth.

In basic college chemistry class, we were taught to bring a solution into a supersaturated state and then cause it to precipitate into a solid. Chemical indicators informed us when the chemical neared the supersaturated liquid point. Then even one solid crystal grain of the same chemical added to the supersaturated liquid at normal temperature in the lab caused the liquid to solidify. We also see various solids form from liquids under other limiting factors such as temperature and pressure. Several examples of this are the sequences of vapor-water-ice and magma-basalt-lava or obsidian. Other occurrences are present in nature under other limiting conditions that God developed into the natural laws by which our world operates.

When the finger of God began precipitating His elemental soup into land, monumental cataclysms must have occurred throughout our planet, if not throughout the universe. The precipitation of the distinctive saturated elements may have been done individually, or more likely, simultaneously worldwide. The results produced the various land-forming complexities spreading over and throughout the earth molding the different rock formations we see today.

Many scientists accept the idea of Pangaea, one early original large continental land mass initially formed but later pulled apart by tectonic forces to drift into the continents we know today on earth's surface. This may be what scripture describes as "the gathering of the waters into one place" and perhaps of the land also. Calling the water in their plurality "seas" may cause dispute. However, that scripture description may merely be speaking of the separation of water within its God-given limits from the formation of land on Creation's Day Three.

The basic rocks formed at that time are what we call igneous rocks in today's geological terms. Problems regarding geological terms are complicated when scientific hypotheses are brought forward without using the Bible as a reference for analysis. For example, The Big Bang Theory prevails in the minds of many non-biblical scientists in their explanation of nature's geological record. That theory entails a fiery beginning of molten rock and elements contrary to the biblical account of a watery beginning. However, the watery beginning presented in scripture, lines up with what we observe in nature around us today. Nature does not make a simplistic appearance, but instead utilizes complex cause and effect to put events into place through the original acts of God. One excellent example is the complex layering of sedimentary rocks with varied types of fossil shellfish intertwined and deposited within sandstones, shales, and invasive igneous rock beds.

Earth's surface is estimated as being around 10+ miles thick. This is significant because the earth is around eight thousand miles in diameter. Of this 10+ miles, geologists identify 95% as igneous rock, sedimentary formations resulting from mud at 4%, sand 0.75%, with 0.25% being calcareous from sea creatures (J. F. Kemp's *A Handbook of Rocks*). First published in 1896, Kemp's seminal book was last updated in 2007. Other information sources vary widely as to the depth and physical breakdown of rock composing the earth's crust, e.g. *Geology and Creation* by Don DeYoung, describes the earth's surface as being 67% igneous rock, 25% metamorphic, and 8% sedimentary. Kemp's book, originally written in 1896, apparently placed metamorphic rocks within the igneous category. The fact that metamorphic rock usually forms when sedimentary rock undergoes transformation through the application of great heat and pressure helps to explain the considerably greater percentage of igneous rock cited by Kemp than by DeYoung.

Disagreement among scientists on such issues as the composition and/or breakdown of the earth's crust is not a significant factor concerning this book's purpose. I personally believe that during God's formative separation of lands and seas, the original land formed from a quickly precipitated matrix separating into igneous, sedimentary, and metamorphic forms of rock, not instantaneously, but over a period of several thousands of years up until the time of the flood.

God's biblical record does indicate a watery beginning. Note 2 Peter 3:5, "For when they maintain this, it escapes their notice that by the word of God *the* heavens existed long ago and *the* earth was formed out of water and by water." Some describe the hypothesis of the *element-soup* beginnings for the earth and universe as water extending upwards throughout the galaxy and universe.

In a speculative view, compaction after precipitation of the chemical *element soup* would have generated great heat in the spherical mass of lands and seas known as our earth. However, this may actually have been accomplished at a much lower temperature and in a shorter time span than indicated by well-meaning geologists ignorant of the Bible. For example, a cool mode of granite rock formation with its sharp-angular formation of the different crystal forms of feldspar, mica and silicates, may have been what happened during the Creation's Day Three. Such sharp-angular mineral formations within granite rock are more conceivably formed under lower temperatures and in a watery base than what is espoused by proponents of higher temperature in a firey beginning.

Primarily that difference concerns the time element involved as well as considerations regarding the effects of a watery base. Secular scientists generally ascribe time spans of billions of years for such rock formation. However, creation scientists use terms ranging from almost instantaneous to days, years, decades or even centuries. The concept describing rapid cooling effects of water in the earth's magma, plus the rapid formation of igneous rocks, shortens the time span required for rock crystal development to days or hours, even for crystal sizes varying from several millimeters to several feet in length.

We have seen that the percentage of dissolved water in the magma, in the form of steam, increases by depth into the earth's interior. At two miles depth, magma holds about 3.7%

water, but at sixty miles depth the dissolved water content reaches 24% (Snelling). Similarly, temperatures increase with depth, ranging from relatively cool on the earth's surface to temperatures between 1300 degrees Fahrenheit and 2200 degrees Fahrenheit as magma changes into the liquid state at eighteen miles depth.

Similarly, there is significance in the water content of the rock as to its cooling effect on the granites, basalts and volcanic rock formed. Surface water has a rapid cooling effect as it flows in and through the rock in formation. For the formation of crystals, the greater the water content, the shorter the cooling time for the estimates provided by creation scientists and matches the six days of creation provided in the Bible's account of creation as covering 1656 years until the flood, or about the year 2300 BC.

Keep in mind my proposal regarding creation's supersaturated state of *element soup* when forming the basic magma making up our earth through rapid precipitation. Rock building of igneous, sedimentary and metamorphic forms continued until the flood came around seventeen hundred years later. And rock formation continues to our present day but under different conditions due to varying environmental changes in our world after the flood.

The significance of this information is the magnitude of the water content and high temperatures of magma near the surface of the earth into depths uncharted by mankind. The Big-Bang Theory does not take into consideration the high water content in earth's magma as indicated by Bible-based scientific creation theories that the earth was formed out of water. Most secular science gurus do not desire to credit God for creation when found in error. Ideally, their reaction should be, "I am beginning to see evidence that there must be a God in the heavens and I must get to know Him." Instead, their more usual response has been, "We may have been found in error this time, but there must be another secular, godless answer to this question."

Angularization of the crystal formation in igneous, granite rocks indicates formation at cooler temperatures compared with hotter flowing basalts forming with lower water content. For example, on the north shore of Lake Superior, the Thompsonite agate residues found amongst the basalts are rounded by nature. Therefore, the higher basalt temperatures and their lower water content were in some way responsible for the lack of angularization in this crystalline type of formation. Even practical observations by non-professional geologists may assist those with other creationist views by pointing to the infinite wisdom of God and the inerrancy of His Bible.

According to Genesis 1:11-13, the initial seed planting by God for the creation of vegetation was completed in the Creation's Day Three: [11]"Then God said, 'Let the earth sprout vegetation: plants yielding seed, *and* fruit trees on the earth bearing fruit after their kind with seed in them'; and it was so. [12]The earth brought forth vegetation, plants yielding seed after their kind, and trees bearing fruit with seed in them, after their kind; and God saw that it was good. [13]There was evening and there was morning, a third day."

In terms of the pre-flood environment, consider Genesis 2:5-6, "[5]Now no shrub of the field was yet in the earth, and no plant of the field had yet sprouted, for the Lord

God had not sent rain upon the earth, and there was no man to cultivate the ground. [6]But a mist used to rise from the earth and water the whole surface of the ground." After the flood, the advent of rain upon the earth changed things with the opening up of the firmament as we know it today. Genesis 9:13-15 adds, "'[13]I set My bow in the cloud, and it shall be for a sign of a covenant between Me and the earth. [14]It shall come about, when I bring a cloud over the earth, that the bow will be seen in the cloud, [15]and I will remember My covenant, which is between Me and you and every living creature of all flesh; and never again shall the water become a flood to destroy all flesh.'"

It is apparent that pre-flood conditions were much different than those we have today. Studies of the supersaturated state provide good explanation for early creation of the world, including earth's atmosphere. The hot-house effect of that atmosphere would have had a profound effect on plant growth for especially the early species of soft ferns and the spore-type vegetation capable of growing profusely and surviving from sustenance obtained directly from the air. The finger of God triggered this growth much as described in the precipitative formation of rock, planting different species after their kind all over the earth, some faster growing than others. The simplest basic types, like ferns, grow profusely in hot-house conditions, producing vast amounts of covering vegetation quickly but interspersed with slower-growing trees and hard, woody shrubs.

The early-world instability of land formation caused wide fluctuations with seas inundating the lands and abundant vegetative growth forming the vast beds of coal we have today throughout our earth. Presumably earthquakes also were quite active like the powerful events we see today, but occurring in the fluid earth, as well as in the seas, in our world's early existence. Minor or major fluctuations of atmospheric pressure, whether occurring directly at God's command, or indirectly and naturally through the laws of nature that God put into place, could be just enough to force the seas and fluid land masses to rise and fall, leaving room for the inundations and recessions of the seas over those newly formed land masses just created by God. The geological rock record of vast coal deposits all over the world indicates great fluctuations of lands frequently inundated by seas.

Coal deposits quickly accumulated from the initial implantation of many vegetation forms resulting from Creation's Day Three until the flood came nearly 1700 years later. At that point, nature's entropy, the trend from order to disorder, had also begun throughout the geological earth. This resulted in the erosive chemical decomposition of soils caused as the vegetative cover rapidly progressed throughout the earth's newly created land mass. The land itself was worn away by erosion caused from the repeated inundation and retreat of the seas amidst the rapidly fluctuating wave action on the earth's surface. Moisture from the atmosphere, as it existed then, was also chemically and physically erosive against the earth's surface. The cycles and processes of entropy and vegetative growth throughout earth's land mass continued until the flood in a physical setting different to what we observe and live in today.

The rising and falling on our globe's newly formed crust was understandably accompanied by atmospheric pressure changes from above, as well as by density changes within the earth and seas. Abundant vegetative deposits were quickly established in the form of huge fern-like trees as evidenced by the clear record of fossil forests in coal seen today, and also visible in other mineral deposits. For example, complete palm fronds approaching thirty feet in height, intact from stem to leaf, have been found at the Gilboa site of New York since the 1920s, as well as on the North America's Pacific Coast near Bellingham, Washington, and on Kodiak Island, Alaska. Coal deposits interspersed with sandstone, shales and limestone, have been found in situ, as well as transported by water to various sites. Washington State's Mt. St. Helens, in its major 1980 eruption, deposited thick forest mats in the bottom of Spirit Lake similar to the waterborne deposits in ancient coal beds. It is only logical that the lighter woody tissue of frond-like, newly created vegetation floated to the surface as similar vegetation did in Spirit Lake during Mt. St. Helen's last major eruption in 1980.

It is very conceivable then that water saturation along with erosive runoff from adjacent lands would cause rafts of vegetation to sink to the bottom and be covered by sediment from other sources. Such processes, occurring and reoccurring over a period covering the 1700 years preceding the great flood accounts for the cyclical deposits of coal and other sedimentary rocks in earth's geological record as we see it today.

These examples are a brief restatement of Day Three of creation as seen in the biblical record, supplemented with evidence from the scientific record. Thankfully, God lets the scientific community gather information for the public domain unbiased by preconceived conclusions as to the meaning of their findings. When the dust clears, valid scientific data stands supportive of a young earth, created by our all-knowing God, as presented in the Holy Bible.

In review, on Creation's Day Three, God started the formation process of earth's rocks and minerals. This was most likely a precipitous effect for the formation of land masses still visible today in somewhat altered form. During Day Three, God also established vegetative coverings for the earth, forming all phylum that we observe today or find in the geologic record through many horizons of rock formations.

Men investigate natural phenomena with inquisitive minds to make our life here on earth more interesting and to reveal more about our Creator. This Creator, God, reveals Himself through all that He has created, including His inspired Holy Word, the Bible. The glories of creation through the Father, Son and Holy Spirit awaken the mind of man to His glory in the Bible, in poetry and in other expressions of His creative beauty expressed throughout time by those who love Him. Deuteronomy 29:29 says, "The secret things belong to the LORD our God, but the things revealed belong to us and to our sons forever, that we may observe all the words of this law." By His law, He established the heavens and the earth. May our Triune, God, the Father, Son and Holy Spirit, continue to reveal the wonders of His world, universe, and very self to all who seek Him, and love Him, and all that He is. May further revelations and understanding of Him occur as we walk in the newness of life He makes available through His Son, Jesus Christ, who lives and reigns forevermore.

For the Beauty of the Earth:
Revelation of Creation's Day Three

In summary regarding the sovereignty of the Creator, Proverbs 8:23-26 says: [23]"'From everlasting I was established, from the beginning, from the earliest times of the earth. [24]When there were no depths I was brought forth, when there were no springs abounding with water. [25]"Before the mountains were settled, before the hills I was brought forth; [26]while He had not yet made the earth and the fields, nor the first dust of the world. Psalms 90:2 adds, "Before the mountains were born or You gave birth to the earth and the world, even from everlasting to everlasting, You are God." Yes, from everlasting to everlasting, God's Wisdom, the Word, Christ, was present in creation, communicating to us. In Isaiah 52:7 that prophet says, "How lovely on the mountains are the feet of him who brings good news, who announces peace and brings good news of happiness, who announces salvation, *and* says to Zion, 'Your God reigns!'"

What brings joy and happiness to these wandering feet? It is God's word shouted from the mountain tops revealed to mankind as in Amos 4:13: "For behold, He who forms mountains and creates the wind and declares to man what are His thoughts, He who makes dawn into darkness and treads on the high places of the earth, the LORD God of hosts is His name."

Just what is this good news? It is knowledge of the God forming the earth on Creation's Day Three and the appearance of all of the mountains and glades resounding with the music of praise for Him as heard in Isaiah 55:12, "For you will go out with joy and be led forth with peace; the mountains and the hills will break forth into shouts of joy before you, and all the trees of the field will clap *their* hands."

The precipitation of rock is generated
In forms considered igneous, metamorphic and sedimented.
Some are precipitated through temperature and pressure.
Others occur through life, death and weather.

Our Holy God set all this in motion,
Setting aside land, sky and oceans,
Plants abound on this land we know,
Created by God for us to grow.

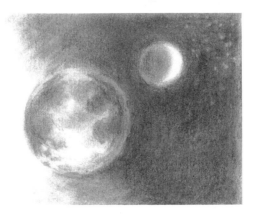

Chapter 8

SUN, MOON AND STARS: CREATION'S DAY FOUR

There is one glory of the sun, and another glory of the moon, and another glory of the stars; for star differs from star in glory.
1 CORINTHIANS 15:41,

Years ago I recall a young boy sitting in the front seat of my car in Minneapolis one spring evening waiting for me to come out of the house and drive him somewhere. I rounded the corner of the house just in time to see him impatiently lay on the horn to make me hurry. At the exact instant that my little friend hit the horn, all of the lights in downtown Minneapolis switched on. The lad looked up, amazed at what he thought he had accomplished. He then beeped my horn again in greater earnest, hoping that perhaps he could turn on more lights, maybe all of the lights in the universe, as darkness overspread the skies.

You and I both know that my little friend did not turn on the lights of the universe that night. I did not either, nor did any man who ever walked this earth. However, God's Son had a primary role in our earth's creation prior to walking the earth as Jesus, the Son of God, son of Mary, born two thousand years ago, who despite His short thirty-three years on earth, lived redemption's glory we have seen and touched. He is now triumphant and risen, returned to the Father, incorruptible to the effects of death forevermore. Prior to walking this earth as a man, He created the lights of the universe for all of us to see, and now reigns beside God the Father, interceding and intervening as the Son of Man and Son of God on behalf of all believers who seek and love Him.

Genesis 1:14-19 records the event: [14]"Then God said, 'Let there be lights in the expanse of the heavens to separate the day from the night, and let them be for signs and for seasons and for days and years; [15]and let them be for lights in the expanse of the heavens to give light on the earth'; and it was so. [16]God made the two great lights, the greater light to govern the day, and the lesser light to govern the night; *He made* the stars also. [17]God placed them in the expanse of the heavens to give light on the earth, [18]and to govern the day and the night, and to separate the light from the darkness; and God saw that it was good. [19]There was evening and there was morning, a fourth day." Reviewing creation's, Day One, Psalms 74:16 states, "Yours is the day, Yours also is the night; You have prepared the light and the sun." Our God turned on all the lights of the universe.

Concerning Creation Days One and Four, Psalm 74 indicates something other than the creation of light, day, and night, on that first day. In addition on Creation's Day Four is the establishment of the sun to furnish wonderful light to the world. Light and darkness were formed on creation Day One as discussed earlier in detail. It is surmised that God may have put everything in place for the grand finale of His six creation days. God's supernatural light shone visibly from Days One to Three, prior to the appearance of the sun, moon and stars which on Day Four were formed as literal luminary bodies. Pre-creation time established systems for the creation of these luminaries able to be perceived within our range of vision.

Many varied lengths of wave technologies are unknown to man, but known to God. There are long and short lengths, from the most minute X-rays to long radio waves, beyond the range of human vision but known and scientifically helpful to man. In fact, more waves are being discovered and utilized all the time. God's creation of matter is beyond human comprehension, but God was also busy prior to His seven creation days getting everything in order for the greatest engineering feat known to mankind.

On Day Four, God stated, "Let there be," and all elements fell into place creating the lights for our earth in the heavens through channels pre-established by Him during pre-creation time. Hebrews 11:3 explains, "By faith we understand that the worlds were prepared by the word of God, so that what is seen was not made out of things which are visible."

Mentioned earlier as the author of "Star Formation and Genesis 1," respected semanticist and linguist, James Stambaugh, M.Div., makes the following remarks concerning, "Let there be." He says, "whether translated 'ex *nihilo*' (out of nothing) or 'de *novo'* (something new), they represent a fundamental change in the object that is 'created.'"

Job 38:4-7 describes the stars as being "alive with the sound of music: ⁴"'Where were you when I laid the foundation of the earth? Tell *Me,* if you have understanding, ⁵Who set its measurements? Since you know. Or who stretched the line on it? ⁶On what were its bases sunk? Or who laid its cornerstone, ⁷when the morning stars sang together and all the sons of God shouted for joy?'" Such passages make me wonder who was there during the placement of the Sun, Moon and Stars. They also make me believe that there were angelic beings alive prior to the six days of creation. The very stars themselves seem alive with some sort of spiritual life beyond our comprehension of the ways and understanding of God and His creation. The Bible tells us that the sun, moon and stars did not exist as the luminaries we're familiar with until Creation's Day Four. Very likely angelic beings existed and were instrumental with God the Father, God, the Son, and God, the Holy Spirit in assisting, preparing and setting up the grand creation of this earth within its universe.

There is a big difference between God the Son (Jesus Christ) and the *sons of God* who apparently were angelic beings prior to Creation's six days. God's Son is called *eternal Father* in this Isaiah 9:6-7 prophetic passage about the Christ: ⁶"For a child will be born to us, a son will be given to us; and the government will rest on His shoulders; and His name will be called Wonderful Counselor, Mighty God, Eternal Father, Prince of Peace. ⁷There will be no end to the increase of *His* government or of peace, on the throne of David and over his kingdom, to establish it and to uphold it with justice and righteousness from then on and forevermore. The zeal of the LORD of hosts will accomplish this."

Genesis 1, John 1, and Hebrews 1, all describe Jesus as being present and responsible for the creation of all things, with all things created by Him, through Him and for Him. Psalms 90:2 adds, [2]"Before the mountains were born or You gave birth to the earth and the world, even from everlasting to everlasting, You are God."

Job 38:7 indicates that some form of angelic beings were present on Creation's Day Four: "When the morning stars sang together and all the sons of God shouted for joy." The Bible also acknowledges angelic beings as pre-existing, but being removed from the angelic and human gene pool, according to the words of Jesus in Luke 20:34-36 when He was questioned regarding marriage following the resurrection from the dead: [34]And Jesus said to them, 'The sons of this age marry and are given in marriage, [35]but those who are considered worthy to attain to that age and the resurrection from the dead, neither marry nor are given in marriage; [36]for they cannot even die anymore, because they are like angels, and are sons of God, being sons of the resurrection.'"

Therefore we see that the sons of God, prior to the birth of Christ through the Virgin Mary, are angelic beings capable of reproducing with humankind. In Genesis 6:4, the Bible says that the offspring of such unions, called Nephilim, were produced by angelic union with the human females of this world: "The Nephilim were on the earth in those days, and also afterward, when the sons of God came in to the daughters of men, and they bore *children* to them. Those were the mighty men who *were* of old, men of renown."

Who all was present at creation? Study indicates that the Father, Son and Holy Spirit were present, as well as possibly a myriad of angelic beings in the form of stars and even angels resembling humans. When the Bible says, "Let us create man in our image," it is usually believed to indicate only the Father, Son and Holy Spirit. However, the understanding communicated to me through scripture is that other angelic beings also existed and were also instrumental in setting the stage for the greatest engineering feat of all time, the creation of the heavens and earth. One thing is for sure: my young friend who turned on the lights of Minneapolis that evening was not there. Neither was any uncreated human, since mankind was not formed until Creation's Day Six as God's crowning masterpiece.

Concerning the existence and function of heavenly bodies, some people ask, "Why are they here?" The more important question is, "Why are we here?" The answer is that our loving and righteous Creator brought everything into existence including us. We know that we exist to bring glory to His name. Exactly how we are to do this may elude some of us, but is an issue to be worked out in each individual life. No man can fully explain a purpose for God's creation or its processes. The Bible tells us that the heaven's luminaries help us as we live upon this earth and perhaps occupy the universe.

First of all, the luminaries are created for light. Jeremiah 31:35 says, "Thus says the LORD, who gives the sun for light by day and the fixed order of the moon and the stars for light by night,... The LORD of hosts is His name."

They are created for seasons. Psalms 104:19 states, "He made the moon for the seasons; the sun knows the place of its setting. Psalms 74:16-17 adds, "Yours is the day, Yours also is the night; You have prepared the light and the sun. [17]You have established all the boundaries of the earth; You have made summer and winter."

God created all the host of heaven, including the binary stars and galaxies, for glory and beauty. Job 9:7-10 declares, [7]"Who commands the sun not to shine, and sets a seal upon the stars; [8]Who alone stretches out the heavens and tramples down the waves of the sea; [9]Who makes the Bear, Orion and the Pleiades, and the chambers of the south; [10]Who does great things, unfathomable, and wondrous works without number." 1 Corinthians 15:41 instructs, "There is one glory of the sun, and another glory of the moon, and another glory of the stars; for star differs from star in glory."

Although the Bible gives little direct mention of navigation, even the most simple world civilizations discovered the use of the sun and stars for navigation and accurate determination of place location in time and space when no other visible landmarks were available to guide them for sailing at sea or crossing a desert. Someday the stars may guide mankind further throughout our galaxy and universe, if it pleases Him.

Was the creation of God's Universe a one-time event? Or Ongoing? Many people consider that creation of the universe as a one-time occurrence. Fast-forwarding to the fall of mankind, We may state, tongue in cheek, that God and His angelic beings have not had a good rest since mankind's fall into sin. One thing is sure, since the fall, mankind has kept God's heavenly host busy in matters concerning eternity. Regarding God's laws and principles concerning operation of our earth, the universe, and possible universes, He is very possibly still busy creating other worlds. The Bible tells us that our God calls each of us by name, individually and personally. He knew us individually when He formed us in our mother's womb and chose us, each one. Salvation is not group therapy. We each come to the Lord singly with our individual hearts doing eternal business with God.

The following scriptures establish that this is also the way God rules His universe: Isaiah 40:26 says, "Lift up your eyes on high and see who has created these stars, the one who leads forth their host by number, He calls them all by name; because of the greatness of His might and the strength of *His* power, not one *of them* is missing." As you see, the wording in this passage is very similar to God's individual calling and choosing of people here on earth for His heavenly kingdom. He treats the very stars as living beings, not as an impersonal scientist naming animals and/or people, nor as geologists or foresters naming earth formations, rocks, ecosystems or trees. God deals with them and names them individually, so as not to lose one of them.

He also has instilled this godly trait into the heart of man when it comes to relating with family and friends during life on earth. Similarly Scripture conveys that God endowed His heavenly host with individual qualities and the purposes of personal touch. Psalms 8:3-4 states, [3]"When I consider Your heavens, the work of Your fingers, the moon and the stars, which You have ordained; [4]What is man that You take thought of him, and the son of man that You care for him?" God's heavenly hosts are mentioned on Day Four of creation in conjunction with His creation of humankind.

The Movie and TV series, *Star Trek*, was sheer fantasy showing man going throughout the universe mining, plundering, saving and destroying as he willed what God has created. In reality, God cares for His creation in a manner similar to His dealings with mankind. Scripture says He placed the heavenly host with His "fingers," conveying His loving thoughtfulness and purpose. Our Savior, Jesus Christ births us into the *Family of God* and shares His creation with us, desiring us who follow Him to understand and administrate all of creation around us by His same principles.

God did not stagnate during the Creation's Day Seven following His six days of creating this universe. Listen to Jesus' reply to the Pharisees in John 5:17 when they accused Him of working on a Sabbath day: "But He answered them, 'My Father is working until now, and I Myself am working.'" We call our Trinitarian God, the Creator; that is His nature and He is still creating. He may be creating new universes and worlds for the further inhabitation of mankind...or for other purposes that He will yet make clear in the future.

One important thing that first needs to be accomplished is the achievement of peace in this world as well as in the individual hearts of men. This is a job best done one person at a time as He gives people understanding and brings us into His kingdom of light. As 2 Corinthians 4:6 confirms, "For God, who said, 'Light shall shine out of darkness,' is the One who has shone in our hearts to give the Light of the knowledge of the glory of God in the face of Christ Jesus."

Many scriptures discuss the permanence of God's created universe. Consider Psalms 148:1-6: [1"]Praise the

LORD! Praise the LORD from the heavens; Praise Him in the heights! [2]Praise Him, all His angels; Praise Him, all His hosts! [3]Praise Him, sun and moon; Praise Him, all stars of light! [4]Praise Him, highest heavens, and the waters that are above the heavens! [5]Let them praise the name of the LORD, for He commanded and they were created. [6]He has also established them forever and ever; He has made a decree which will not pass away."

However, scriptures like Revelation 21:1 include qualifying comments regarding this permanence: "Then I saw a new heaven and a new earth; for the first heaven and the first earth passed away,..." The first law of thermodynamics in physics, the law of conservation of matter and energy, states that nothing (no *matter*) can be created or destroyed. Something remains in changed form, no matter the process, just as when we become Christians and are changed as all things become new. As 2 Corinthians 5:17 states, "Therefore if anyone is in Christ, *he is* a new creature; the old things passed away; behold, new things have come."

The shocking phrase *"Burn baby burn!"* came out of the racial riots of the early 1960s. That phrase in conjunction with The Big Bang Theory seems to predict a continuous repetitive ending and re-beginning to our universe. Yet regarding worldly counsel, the Bible says in Isaiah 47:13, "You are wearied with your many counsels; let now the astrologers, those who prophesy by the stars, those who predict by the new moons, stand up and save you from what will come upon you." In other words, when facing cataclysmic circumstances, worldly counsel provides little hope or lasting help.

In contrast, consider the hope found in the Bible. According to 2 Peter 3:10, "But the day of the Lord will come like a thief, in which the heavens will pass away with a roar and the elements will be destroyed with intense heat, and the earth and its works will be burned up." This word picture makes the scripture verses from Isaiah 6 seem appropriate as the prophet cries out, "Woe is me, for I am a man of unclean lips." But the passage in 2 Peter goes further: [13]"But according to His promise we are looking for new heavens and a new earth, in which righteousness dwells. [14]Therefore, beloved, since you look for these things, be diligent to be found by Him in peace, spotless and blameless, [15]and regard the patience of our Lord *as* salvation; just as also our beloved brother Paul, according to the wisdom given him, wrote to you."

Woe to each of us caught in this dilemma. It's as though we are still men or women of unclean lips going from the frying pan into the fire! Yet, there must be a way out of the predicament we find ourselves in. Joel 2:12-14 says, [12]"Yet even now," declares the LORD, 'Return to Me with all your heart, and with fasting, weeping and mourning; [13]and rend your heart and not your garments.' Now return to the LORD your God, for He is gracious and compassionate, slow to anger, abounding in lovingkindness and relenting of evil. [14]Who knows whether He will *not* turn and relent and leave a blessing behind Him?"

When panic and fear of evil abound, God's grace more than abounds. He delights in giving a blessing instead of a curse. How can we proceed? What can we do? Isaiah 40:31 answers, "Yet those who wait for the LORD will gain new strength; they will mount up *with* wings like eagles, they will run and not get tired, they will walk and not become weary."

God's word instructs us to wait upon the Lord. Be calm. Wait a minute. It's not over until it's over. What do we fear? Daniel 12:3 promises, "Those who have insight will shine brightly like the brightness of the expanse of heaven, and those who lead the many to righteousness, like the stars forever and ever." Actually, any of us who receive God's message and share it are preachers of Christ. 1 Timothy 4:16 says, "Pay close attention to yourself and to your teaching; persevere in these things, for as you do this you will ensure salvation both for yourself and for those who hear you." Acts 4:12 adds, "And there is salvation in no one else; for there is no other name (Christ Jesus) under heaven that has been given among men by which we must be saved."

Concerning coming testing times, our Lord indicates certain things: Luke 21:33 "Heaven and earth will pass away, but My words will not pass away." Isaiah 34:4 states, "And all the host of heaven will wear away, and the sky will be rolled up like a scroll; all their hosts will also wither away as a leaf withers from the vine, or as *one* withers from the fig tree." In Matthew 24:36-39, Jesus shared these words with His disciples: [36]"But of that day and hour no one knows, not even the angels of heaven, nor the Son, but the Father alone. [37]For the coming of the Son of Man will be just like the days of Noah. [38]For as in those days before the flood they were eating and drinking, marrying and giving in marriage, until the day that Noah entered the ark, [39]and they did not understand until the flood came and took them all away; so will the coming of the Son of Man be."

When viewed through the eyes of God and Holy Scriptures, no end-time scenario appears ominous or threatening. Instead, His words bring comfort. Get into God's Word, His words and principles and seek what lasts eternally, including life for ourselves, our family and friends. When the Bible says, "Eat the Scroll," it means we are to incorporate God's holy word in both Old and New Testaments into the very fabric of our souls and lives. We assimilate this until it becomes part and fiber of us, and then observe and teach what is written with all diligence for our own salvation and for that of those who hear us, hopefully including all of our family and friends. Deuteronomy 29:29 promises, "The secret things belong to the LORD our God, but the things revealed belong to us and to our sons forever, that we may observe all the words of this law."

Like Frank Sinatra's song, research scientists often think, "I did it my way," not acknowledging God's involvement in creation. However, finite man had better ask himself, where does my capacity for receiving any and all inspiration and revelation come from? From God? Or...? Consider the social sciences and their sources for credibility—like psychology, for example. Do its principles contain absolutes and wisdom established for man from God's rules in the Bible, leading to peace and life? Or are they permissive, non-absolute situational ethics based on psychological principles containing gradualism and explaining away sins like lust, greed and debauchery which lead to death? Exponents of both systems claim that they work depending on the life goals that respective practitioners embrace. However, Matthew 6:33 instructs, "seek first His kingdom and His righteousness, and all these things will be added to you."

God's revelations can be used for good or evil, leading to life or to death. Like nuclear power, the misapplication of God's laws leads to dire consequences when used contrary to the good that God intended. For this reason God should be acknowledged and honored concerning His revelations to mankind. If we revel in the human mindset, claiming "I did it my way," and for myself, we are on the verge of serious trouble. However, when God's revelations are used for good as He intended, wonderful results occur for us personally and for those with whom we're involved. Choose the good offered in the Bible and, as God's word says, "all these things shall be added unto you." When we can say, "I did it God's way," we're at least halfway home and free from the burdens that tend to entangle us. How do we do it God's way? The very best way is to become familiar with His word, the Bible, plus learn from excellent teachers of His Word.

Concerning creation, ask anyone, believer or unbeliever, "Just who turned on the lights?" Many may answer: "You see, there was this big explosion billions, no hundreds of billions of years ago, and 'whammo,' here we be." Ridiculous isn't it? Those with understanding will answer, "Why it was God, the Creator, who made all things." That is a better answer. However, then it is good to inquire, "Which God?" just to make sure that they are crediting the Triune God of the universe as portrayed in the Bible, made up of the Father, the Son and the Holy Spirit. But don't even stop there. Explain what the Bible teaches about this Trinitarian God. For as His creation, we are invited to learn all we can about Him and

His holy ways. Besides reading God's word, we can learn more about Him in most Christian churches or in book stores anywhere on earth. May this gospel-based poem help get you started, as it describes some of the wonderful attributes in our "Father of lights in whom is no shadow of turning:"

Through the Son the starry, heavenly host is created,
Look up and live His love is emanated.
His life abounds from man to man unabated,
By His command His word is reinstated.

The sun, moon and stars exemplify God's glory;
Their purpose is to tell the old, old story.
From Him alone atonement is given;
His Son lived and died that we might be forgiven.

Chapter 9

SEA CREATURES AND BIRDS: CREATION'S DAY FIVE

Then God said, "Let the waters teem with swarms of living creatures,and let birds fly above the earth in the open expanse of the heavens." GENESIS 1:20,

Remember "Dino," the cuddly purple dinosaur? The phrase said, "He isn't hairy, nor is he scary." However, on the Creation's Day Five, God did create some scary types of dinosaurs. He also created fish, mollusks, and leviathans in the seas, and birds to fly around the heavens. His creation process and sequence is recorded in the Bible, as well as being visible in the fossil record containing examples of some creatures who still move in our midst today.

Genesis 1:20-23 adds, [20]"Then God said, 'Let the waters teem with swarms of living creatures, and let birds fly above the earth in the open expanse of the heavens.' [21]God created the great sea monsters and every living creature that moves, with which the waters swarmed after their kind, and every winged bird after its kind; and God saw that it was good. [22]God blessed them, saying, 'Be fruitful and multiply, and fill the waters in the seas, and let birds multiply on the earth.' [23]There was evening and there was morning, a fifth day."

Let us discuss the fertility of early Earth. In the years preceding the flood the makeup of the earth, air and seas were understandably completely different than what we have known since the great deluge occurring around 2300 BC. Based on understanding the Bible to be the infallible word of God as supported by scientific studies and disciplines, let us build on the explanation of the seas consisting of *element soup*, as discussed earlier, with the atmosphere being a relatively humid and steamy hothouse.

The combination of *element soup* in the seas surrounded by hot, humid atmosphere were the conditions present when God introduced living creatures into the seas and birds into the air of this created world. Therefore, on Creation's Day Three, His stage was set when land precipitated from the *element soup* of earth's watery beginnings, along with the introduction of plant life onto earth's surface and phytoplankton into the seas. On Creation's Day Four, all living things were warmed and incubated for growth through the addition of the sun, and influenced by heavenly bodies within our galaxy.

The geological phenomena observed on earth today become a reliable story book to read the earth's past. The super-saturated condition of Earth following the formation of land but prior to the great flood is the logical explanation for understanding the significant rapid growth of sea creatures witnessed by the presence of calcareous deposits hundreds of feet thick in the white cliffs of Dover, England, and extensive shellfish fossil limestone deposits visible elsewhere throughout our world today. God works beyond the limits of any box imposed by human thought. He works beyond anything we can comprehend as made evident by His miraculous events in the Bible further confirmed by historical and archaeological records.

Consider this modern-day evidence. In 1988 the Zebra Mussel, an invasive bi-valve mollusk from Eastern Europe, was accidentally introduced into the Great Lakes by way of ballast discharge from foreign ships navigating U.S. waters. In the early years of this invasion, only the occasional mussel was found on a piece of driftwood, or stuck to the bottom of a boat. However, through rapid multiplication of this invasive species without compensating predatory action of other species to limit their growth, the bottom of the Great Lakes rapidly accumulated serious and annoying amounts of shell sediment. This created problems on recreational beaches as well as having a suffocating effect on native mollusks in Great Lakes waterways. Zebra Mussels have the reproductive capacity of 1,000,000 offspring each per single year. They thrive on phytoplankton, zooplankton and even some pollutants in the lakes, which in turn clears particles suspended in the lakes at the expense of existing native species of fish and other aquatic creatures and vegetation feeding in the Great Lakes biosphere. In just twenty years' time a significant amount of shellfish has accumulated and is a considerable nuisance problem in one of our world's major waterways.

Now, try to envision this earth in pre-flood conditions where similar elements and phytoplankton and zooplankton nutrients were rapidly growing throughout the new world's waterways. Imagine Creator God placing numerous mollusk species throughout those seas, causing them to swarm through the rich, watery world of Creation's Day Five but without the balancing control of predatory species. The Genesis account describes "swarms of living creatures multiplying throughout the seas after their kind." Readers who think that this description of swarming species might be exaggerated should consider today's invasion of the Zebra Mussel as a valid case in point. This initially insignificant limited species is swarming out of control in our world today.

The Bible presents a similar example of *swarming* during Israel's forty years wandering in the wilderness. In Exodus 16:13-15 we read: [13]"So it came about at evening that the quails came up and covered the camp, and in the morning there was a layer of dew around the camp. [14]When the layer of dew evaporated, behold, on the surface of the wilderness there was a fine flake-like thing, fine as the frost on the ground. [15]When the sons of Israel saw *it,* they said to one another, 'What is it?' for they did not know what it was. And Moses said to them, 'It is the bread which the LORD has given you to eat.'"

In Psalms 78:24-29, the Bible provides an additional illustration: [24]"He rained down manna upon them to eat and gave them food from heaven. [25]Man did eat the bread of angels; He sent them food in abundance. [26]He caused the east wind to blow in the heavens and by His power He directed the south wind. [27]When He rained meat upon them like the dust, even winged fowl like the sand of the seas, [28]then He let *them* fall in the midst of their camp, round about their dwellings. [29]So they ate and were well filled, and their desire He gave to them."

Our Creator sometimes greatly multiplies the effects of what appears to be natural phenomena to make them miraculous events. Additional examples are the ten plagues on Egypt leading to Israel's ultimate exodus from that nation. In Matthew 14, as well as in the other Gospel locations, Jesus miraculously fed five thousand men (not counting women and children) from five loaves of bread and two fishes. He blessed and broke this food, passing it to His disciples, having them in turn bless and distribute, until it eventually reached all and fed all of the hungry people gathered there. In fact, after eating and being satisfied, those present gathered up twelve basketsful of abundant leftovers.

The reason these miraculous events are considered as examples of *swarming* is that they did not appear instantly from nothing. Instead they had an original source that appeared to emerge from a seed (or substance) but then transformed by massive divine multiplication. This seems to be the same effect that God's original life seeds had in the fertile seas providing the basic building blocks of calcareous and cretaceous matter seen today in thick limestone deposits found throughout the known world. What took place during twenty years in Lake Michigan with the Zebra Mollusk is child's play compared to what God began on Creation's Day Five continuing until the great flood at approximately 2300 BC., or 1656 years later.

Next let us examine Earth's early historical geological eras. The Precambrian Period is the era geologists identify as that preceding God bringing life to this planet. In the subsequent Cambrian period, geologists first observe mollusks and shellfish. The Bible explains that the land base and its vegetative covering were formed during Creation's Day Three. Shellfish were created on Creation's Day Five prior to the extensive spread of the vegetation created during Creation's Day Three but before land-based vegetation was inundated by seas. This suggests a period of high growth for all animal and vegetable life during and from the six days of creation until the time of the flood, about 1656 years after creation, according to the biblical record.

Earlier in this book, we established that the time sequencing of Creation's six days is small when measured as six 24-hour days. Both semantics and linguistics regarding "day," Hebrew *yom,* and the 24-hour day were explained and discussed in the sequence concerning the early formation of our earth.

The Carboniferous Period, the peak of vegetative coal deposits, succeeds the Cambrian.

It might appear out of sequence according to the geological time lines for Creation's Days Three and Five, but that is due to my hypothesis regarding extensive deposition of life remains in the seas accompanied by rapid stratification of rock formations during the short time span of those six days enabling everything in creation to appear to be created simultaneously.

We know that vegetation appeared in Day Three, luminary bodies in Day Four, and sea and bird life in Day Five. Note that in Day Five with the existence of sea and bird life, our Creator treated conscionable creatures differently than vegetative life in that he "blessed them" and commanded to be "fruitful and multiply." Although these creatures are not created in the image of God, as man is, they are endowed with the gift of life awareness.

Further interesting information concerning Creation's events comes to us through the study of Geology and Theology. Although my knowledge of both fields is rudimentary, it is not hard to pursue correlation of different rock strata formations worldwide. Those doing so will realize that text book analysis on a worldwide basis is virtually impossible if God is taken out of the equation. The process of classifying various stratums of marine life mixed with terrestrial sedimentation should not be labeled insignificant. Knowledge of the orderly classification of different rock strata has helped locate many different valuable rock, mineral and petroleum products in our world today. Where the problem begins is when educators try to explain the orderliness of the sequence of marine animal deposition without including God in the creation process.

Years ago my historical geology class questioned our instructor about the correlation and sequencing of the specific sea creature identifiers used for the geological classifications of sedimentary rocks worldwide. He answered that it is a mystery often contradicted by differing sedimentation patterns throughout the world. He added that some key specie identifiers are missing worldwide in strata considered to be of similar geological age. Furthermore, the time sequences used by most geologists for dating different strata are inconsistent. That is, older indicated stratums are not necessarily found at the bottom of rock sequence formations as expected. Often, younger and older indicators are reversed in their sequence of stratification.

Other fossils used for rock classification within differing geological ages confuse things by popping up continually as living fossils nullifying explanations of the aging hypothesis found in today's geology books. Yet the short life span and high reproduction rate for mollusks and other shell fish explains the immense hundreds of feet thick deposits of these creatures extending from Day Five of the creation until the flood. It appears that this rapid growth rate pattern ceased at the time of the flood.

People often ask if there is a connection between sea monsters and birds. I once read an interesting secular scientific article entitled, "Whatever happened to the dinosaurs?" The answer given was, "They are still living among us in the form of birds." Although this answer initially may sound ludicrous, the author used good logic to reach his conclusion, logic confirming the biblical explanation that they were formed on the same day, Creation's Day Five. The slow growth of both species caused them to begin showing up in the geological record in noticeable numbers at about the same time. There is little evidence of both birds and dinosaurs existing as land-based creatures prior to the flood largely due to the atmosphere's decaying effects on their dead, exposed bodies. In contrast, water burial, is more conducive to good fossil preservation among rapidly-reproducing sea creatures such as mollusks and some fish.

The fossil record is generally quite scarce on birds. Some evidence is there, but it is often difficult due to poor-quality fossilization of their rapidly deteriorating body surface coverings to determine whether what the paleontologists are calling birds contained skin or feathers? God created dinosaurs (no matter how small) after their kind and birds after their kind. They did not cross over, and they never will.

Scientists say that dinosaurs began appearing in the geological record during the Jurassic Period and went into extinction at the beginning of the Quaternary Period in the Pleistocene. Geologists estimate the length of time from the Jurassic to the Pleistocene as 208 million years. The Pleistocene Period appears to be the end of the time of the dinosaurs and correlates with the time of the flood. Mollusks appear in the Cambrian Period matching the beginning of Creation's Day Five. However, geologists estimate the time from the beginning of the appearance of sea life in the form of mollusks from the Cambrian Period to the Pleistocene and the time of the flood at 500 million years. According to the Bible, Creation's Day Five is the creation day for all sea life. Creation's six days until the flood are estimated as being 1656 years based on the biblical records and the scientific information amassed by creation scientists—not the 500 million years theorized by those professing evolution.

It is conceivable that more slowly-reproducing mammals and dinosaurs would gradually start showing up in the geological record until their maximum density at the time of the flood, which was also interestingly the time of their demise. The Pleistocene Epoch, at the beginning of the Quaternary Period, is commonly estimated as the time of the demise of the dinosaurs which correlates with about 2300 BC, the time of the flood and the beginning of the biosphere as we know it today. However, even today the age of the dinosaurs has not yet ended. There also continue to be rumored sightings and even photographs of sea monsters such as the Loch Ness monster in Scotland, the well-documented Ogopogo in British Columbia, Canada, etc.

The Book of Job is usually considered the oldest book of the Bible. It is possible that Job's civilization existed prior to the flood due to clear descriptions in chapters 40 and 41 of the Book of Job of what appear to be dinosaurs. However many theologians propose instead that Job was contemporary with the patriarchs Abraham, Isaac, and Jacob. No matter what age the experts choose as suitable for Job, the fact is that some of the sea monsters and dinosaurs God created on Creation's Day Five existed in Job's day, and in ours. For example, Job described a behemoth which appears to be a dinosaur, possibly a Triceratops, as evidenced by this description in Job 40:15-19: "'Behold now, Behemoth, which I made as well as you; he eats grass like an ox. [16]Behold now, his strength in his loins and his power in the muscles of his belly. [17]He bends his tail like a cedar; the sinews of his thighs are knit together. [18]His bones are tubes of bronze; his limbs are like bars of iron. [19]He is the first of the ways of God; let his maker bring near his sword." Interestingly, the Triceratops is considered to be one of the last survivors of the dinosaurs originating from the Cretaceous period. Significantly, this is also the period beginning the accumulation of sea life, matching Creation's Day Five.

Other ancient creatures, called leviathan in Job, appear to be giant crocodiles which still exist today though in smaller bodily form. In Job 41:1-11 God asks: [1]"'Can you draw out Leviathan with a fishhook? Or press down his tongue with a cord? ²Can you put a rope in his nose or pierce his jaw with a hook? ³Will he make many supplications to you, or will he speak to you soft words? ⁴Will he make a covenant with you? Will you take him for a servant forever? ⁵Will you play with him as with a bird, or will you bind him for your maidens? ⁶Will the traders bargain over him? Will they divide him among the merchants? ⁷Can you fill his skin with harpoons, or his head with fishing spears? ⁸Lay your hand on him; remember the battle; you will not do it again! ⁹Behold, your expectation is false; will you be laid low even at the sight of him? ¹⁰No one is so fierce that he dares to arouse him; who then is he that can stand before Me? ¹¹Who has given to Me that I should repay *him?* Whatever is under the whole heaven is Mine.'"

There also appears to be a vivid description of the armor-plated Thyreophorans dinosaur family with plates on its back and belly in Job 41:12-25, along with fire-breathing dragons from the mid-Jurassic Period: ¹²"I will not keep silence concerning his limbs, or his mighty strength, or his orderly frame. ¹³Who can strip off his outer armor? Who can come within his double mail? ¹⁴Who can open the doors of his face? Around his teeth there is terror. ¹⁵*His* strong scales are *his* pride, shut up *as with* a tight seal. ¹⁶One is so near to another that no air can come between them. ¹⁷They are joined one to another; they clasp each other and cannot be separated. ¹⁸His sneezes flash forth light, and his eyes are like the eyelids of the morning. ¹⁹Out of his mouth go burning torches; sparks of fire leap forth. ²⁰Out of his nostrils smoke goes forth as *from* a boiling pot and *burning* rushes. ²¹His breath kindles coals, and a flame goes forth from his mouth. [22]In his neck lodges strength, and dismay leaps before him. [23]The folds of his flesh are joined together, firm on him and immovable. [24]His heart is as hard as a stone, even as hard as a lower millstone. [25]When he raises himself up, the mighty fear; because of the crashing they are bewildered.'"

Sea monsters and birds lived in the days of Job and may have corresponding residuals in today's world. Consider ancient stories arising from more recent European, Scandinavian, or Chinese times pertaining to fire-breathing dragons. According to the book of Job, such creatures may have actually existed prior to our ancestors becoming civilized. Climate changes before or after the flood may have caused their extinction instantly or gradually as those changes became unable to support their life form. Around the time of the flood, huge temperature changes are recorded through biological indicators in both flora and fauna in the geological columns.

Apparently water-based mammals were also formed during the time when the Bible describes leviathan, because the whale is another of the sea creatures fitting this classification. In Psalms 104:24-26 we read: [24]"O LORD, how many are Your works! In wisdom You have made them all; the earth is full of Your possessions. [2]There is the sea, great and broad, in which are swarms without number, animals both small and great. [26]There the ships move along, *and* Leviathan, which You have formed to sport in it."

Next, consider the insects formed at the same time that their environment was created. Created on Day Three, vegetation logically included the insects common to the type of species within their environment. It is probable that water-borne insects were also formed on Creation's Day Five. Everything necessary to feed earth's creatures, whether fish, mollusks, sea monsters, birds, or small or great mammals, was available on Creation's Day Six.

The larger sea creatures, sea monsters and birds discussed are generally much slower-growing than much more quickly-reproducing shellfish, resulting in only a few such sea creatures showing up in lower rock deposits. Compared to faster-growing mollusks, the slower growth of large sea creatures greatly limits their appearance in limestone, shale and sandstone deposits. Some of these creatures do occasionally thrive on land but are rarely fossilized due to the deterioration and decay process their bodies undergo in our atmosphere.

Fish show up profusely in the sedimentary record due to their comparatively rapid growth with hundreds or thousands of offspring simultaneously hatching in the form of eggs. We may conclude that the majority of fossilized fish are a result of catastrophic mud burial caused by the extreme upheaval of adjacent land masses followed by erosion.

The famous index fossil fish, Coelacanth, was estimated to have lived 300 million years ago in the upper Paleozoic or lower Mesozoic Era. However, several times in recent years this fish has been found in great depths off of the coast of Madagascar with no indicated change in its biological appearance, makeup, or taxonomy. This amazing evidence of what was believed to have been one of the world's oldest fish has compromised and challenged the geological column necessary to believe both the Old Age date for earth's creation, and for the theory of evolution.

Therefore the scientific record indicates that the hand of our Creator planted all sea creatures in the fertile ocean according to His divine plan, as the Bible says, in order to reproduce and multiply upon the earth. God prepared the world stage, making it habitable for the survival of all creatures and the life of mankind, to fulfill His purposes. Creation reveals the joy and beauty in the heart of God, and in His Son, Jesus Christ, Creator of both heavens and earth as expressed in Revelation 4:11: "You are worthy, our Lord and God, to receive glory and honor and power, for you created all things, and by your will they were created and have their being."

Stratigraphic evidence in the geological column also makes it very reasonable that God planted the seeds of His creation in fertile seas in a multi-faceted complexity of life forms. These varied from simple diatoms to complex sea mammals, all with differing longevities and reproductive capabilities. This in turn resulted in some species and life varieties multiplying faster than others, plus permitted some intertwining among them, further complicating the deposition strata sedimentary record.

Varied mollusks and shellfish, representing differing ecological niches, appear in vast amounts by individual or intertwining species as the planted seeds overlapped or were planted simultaneously according to God's wisdom. Yet higher slower-reproducing species also found within rapidly accumulating sedimentary deposits, but on a limited basis depending on specific deposition conditions. For example, the normal death of say a species of fish may rarely be found in rapidly accumulating deposits of shellfish deposited in limestone. However, the same species of fish may be found in abundance in the cataclysmic deposition formed by the violent upheaval of a nearby land mass and subsequent erosion when fish are rapidly buried in fossilized shale or sandstone deposits of considerable depth.

Fossils of land animals and birds are understandably extremely rare due to their reproductive cycles being slower and their death not subject to natural burial in sea deposits. Similarly, slowly-reproducing birds, mammals and dinosaurs, whether residing on the land or in seas, are not normally subjected to the cataclysmic burial that often overtook sea creatures until the time of the great flood. Even during the flood, fossil deposits of land-foraging creatures were rare due to the unique circumstances necessary to place them together in the same location, time, and depth to make a deposit as significant as the Dinosaur National Parks found in parts of Colorado and Utah. Instead, most of the time, land creatures like birds and mammals common to our land environment, die and decay before petrifaction or fossilization can occur.

The investigative tendency of scientists to call everything evolutionary over millions and billions of years is contrary to God's Word, the Bible. Although theories can be used for good when based on sensible and logical foundations, room has to be made for the miraculous intervention of God in the creation process. There are mysteries in this world that mankind will never unravel in our lifetimes due to the fact that God does not choose to reveal them all to us here and now. Remember, Deuteronomy 29:29 says, "The secret things belong to the LORD our God, but the things revealed belong to us and to our sons forever, that we may observe all the words of this law."

Instead, the Bible's purpose is to make us "wise unto salvation." This it admirably does through the wisdom provided in both the Old and New Testaments. The Bible leads us to Christ and His redemptive gift, cancelling our sins, through His death and resurrection. Although the Bible was not intended to be a science book, it provides important and accurate information. No scientist should enter the investigative field without considering its wisdom. Trying to unravel the meaning within God's creation without utilizing the wisdom and beauty of His Holy Word is like going from one winter to the next without letting ourselves be renewed by spring and summer growth and then blessed by fall's harvest and beauty before entering another period of winter's rest. There is a special beauty in winter, too. Mankind needs the contrast between stark winter months and spring's vibrant emergence. Observing and enjoying nature, without considering its Creator, is like choosing to live only in winter, thereby remaining in dreariness and darkness.

John 1:3-5 says, [3]"All things came into being through Him, and apart from Him nothing came into being that has come into being. [4]In Him was life, and the life was the Light of men. [5]The Light shines in the darkness, and the darkness did not comprehend it."

Swarms of birds crowd the skies,
Fish and sea monsters swim side by side,
Mollusks and plankton fill the seas,
Guided by God's hand for all to see.

Jesus fed the hungry masses,
Miraculously fed by mouth and classes,
His word is alive to all who read,
Feeding us who will believe.

Chapter 10

LIVING CREATURES: CREATION'S DAY SIX

For every beast of the forest is Mine, the cattle on a thousand hills... PSALMS 50:10

God set genetic bounds for all of creation after their kind. However, since mankind's fall into sin, abnormalities have developed physically and genetically in various life forms. Kinds do not cross kinds. Diversity within kinds creates sterility amongst species, as when horses breed with donkeys and produce sterile mules. More will be said about that soon. Similarly, God has placed dietary limits on life within His creation, including animal life and mankind as well, subject to the changes implemented at His discretion. Conservation management and good life stewardship were mandated by God in the beginning. The results of man's stewardship to date have been discouraging to most conservation-minded people, although there have been some successes.

Genesis 1:24-31 reads: [24]"Then God said, 'Let the earth bring forth living creatures after their kind: cattle and creeping things and beasts of the earth after their kind'; and it was so. [25]God made the beasts of the earth after their kind, and the cattle after their kind, and everything that creeps on the ground after its kind; and God saw that it was good. [26]Then God said, 'Let Us make man in Our image, according to Our likeness; and let them rule over the fish of the sea and over the birds of the sky and over the cattle and over all the earth, and over every creeping thing that creeps on the earth.' [27]God created man in His own image, in the image of God He created him; male and female He created them. [28]God blessed them; and God said to them, 'Be fruitful and multiply, and fill the earth, and subdue it; and rule over the fish of the sea and over the birds of the sky and over every living thing that moves on the earth.' [29]Then God said, 'Behold, I have given you every plant yielding seed that is on the surface of all the earth, and every tree which has fruit yielding seed; it shall be food for you; [30]and to every beast of the earth and to every bird of the sky and to everything that moves on the earth which has life, *I have given* every green plant for food'; and it was so. [31]God saw all that He had made, and behold, it was very good. And there was evening and there was morning, the sixth day."

In the Bible when God speaks of creating plants and animals "after their kind," He is describing boundaries set in nature created by Himself that are not to be transgressed. Evolutionists would have us believe that all of creation arose from primeval ooze and eventually over billions of years became alive and branched into myriad forms of life.

In the animal world, what God calls "kinds" should not be confused with form diversity. Different kinds are described in the Genesis text as cattle, creeping things, etc. This indicates different kinds or species existing within the wide parameter of "cattle," such as sheep, cows, cats, dogs, these being domestic forms of differing "kinds." Other "kinds" may be giraffes, lions, deer, buffalo, which are wild forms of differing "kinds." Additional "kinds" may be crawling things such as snakes and types of reptiles, or lowly kinds such as mice, squirrels, and hamsters in the rodent groups. These are all animals within which kinds exist that cannot interbreed and reproduce.

Some obvious non-breeding kind of examples are a giraffe with a lion—impossible; an ape with a man—impossible; or a cow with a goat—impossible. You might ask, "Wait a minute, what about the horse and the donkey breeding to produce the mule?" Although the horse and donkey are of the same general "kind," they have lost their reproductivity due to diversity, so the mule cannot reproduce. This loss is not uncommon within nature's diversity. Much change is also evident throughout today's world with genetic diversity accounting for the many differing species we see around us. For example, one species of seagulls, with shared common genetic makeup, developed separate travel patterns between the east and west coasts of the Americas. Though of a similar kind, this physical separation, the segregation of their once common genetic makeup, eventually caused them to lose their interchangeable reproductive capabilities, resulting in different species within their same kind. This same criteria is used when breeding within the species of any single kind. For example, consider the dog. Some dog species are so small they can be put in a teacup. Yet you would have trouble containing others in a pickup.

To obtain specific knowledge, experimentation between kinds is often necessary This has been proven in nearly all meaningful scientific discoveries made by mankind. Think of the thousands of test trials conducted by Edison before he found the solution permitting invention of the light bulb. Serious scientific research and experimentation is a given by God, and necessary in the name of progress when conducted with the proper moral integrity for mankind's benefit. On the extreme opposite end of the spectrum are the scientific experiments conducted by Hitler's Nazi party with absolutely no moral standards or integrity. To the horror of the entire world, these criminal experiments took the lives of many people incarcerated in Hitler's camps. These monstrous unethical experiments were designed to establish cruel subjection over those under Nazi domination.

Yet many species are propagated and enhanced through breeding, pollination and grafting within the parameters of their kind for the benefit of mankind. For example, differing species of fruit, grains and vegetables are enhanced through pollination to develop characteristics favorable to other cultures and countries in differing climate and/or social conditions. The same is true of domestic animals raised under varying conditions in differing countries as dictated by the needs of their respective population and environment.

However, not all experimental "improvements" are beneficial. These must be conducted with great care, keeping the well-being of the animal and society in mind. Today some dogs are bred not for survival, but for someone's interpretation of what qualities a good show dog should exhibit, even if it may eventually lead to the extinction of that species. For example, some species of bulldogs are selectively bred to enhance appearance while decreasing their natural characteristics for survival. On the other hand, during the last century, experimentation with wheat and rice has enhanced the growth of far improved species for impoverished agrarian communities. Similarly, the cross-grafting and pollinating of fruit trees has resulted in some spectacular new species being available for our dinner tables. Apples are cross-pollinated between species to produce varieties more desirable in appearance, taste, etc. Great examples for specific and differing world climatic zones include Red Jonathans, Fuji, and Honeycrisp.

Consider the selective breeding of cattle to produce more milk than was previously thought possible. Similarly, turkey cross-breeding provides more meat poundage per bird today than ever before. All of these accomplishments have been done through various aspects of pollination, grafting or selective breeding without the addition of the chemically-induced changes so often proving harmful to animals and humans.

Although genetic design and manipulation is increasingly utilized today, it should probably not be pursued due to man's limited wisdom and knowledge compared to the plans and designs of God. Some experimentation in the field of genetics should raise eyebrows concerning morality and ethics. For man to get involved in genetic design might be comparable to giving a child barely old enough to crawl a carload of dynamite to play with, along with a box of friction-activated matches. Such experimentations are obviously contrary to God's laws, and we should impose some plain common-sense restrictions on ourselves for safety's sake. Consider early experimentation done to cattle feed combining animal proteins with plants to produce meatier beef. This development was stopped due to findings showing that the results would be harmful to human consumption, and detrimental to cattle. At the present time, hormonal growth stimulants are under close scrutiny due to possible extremely negative effects carried through the food chain to humans as well as to cattle. Sadly, if man pursues genetic experimentation outside of God's parameters, the results could make Mary Shelley's "Frankenstein" fiction story look like reality.

Stem cell research, another controversial scientific topic, appears popular in the eyes of today's medical and scientific professions, as well as in the eyes of the public. Indeed, some adult stem cell research has appeared promising, indicating inroads toward success. For the most part, such experiments are conducted by those revering life, so the results do not appear to be contrary to the laws of God. However, fetal stem cell research has not yet produced anything beneficial to mankind, and in fact is detrimental since it requires the life of a human being that once had a future on earth. This potential young life made up of fetal cells is sacrificed for one whose aged life may be only temporarily enhanced or extended, and this is highly questionable at best. Indeed, We should question the morality of any scientific research requiring the life or torment of the creature being experimented with in the name of benefiting humanity. Such irresponsibility is contrary to God's laws, but also goes against rational sense and sound reasoning. If scientists may pursue adult stem cell research involving no loss of life—Yes! But pursue fetal stem cell research, requiring the loss of life—No!

By studying the fathers of discovery in scientific fields, it seems that nothing truly beneficial to man has been discovered outside of the researchers conducting their work for the glory of God. If a scientist desires success, it would be best if his research is done with a pen in one hand and a Bible in the other. Much eternal truth is found within the covers of the Bible, along with the guidelines needed to live a beneficial life for ourselves, our families, and mankind.

Isaiah 45:18 states, "For thus says the LORD, who created the heavens (He is the God who formed the earth and made it, He established it *and* did not create it a waste place, *but* formed it to be inhabited), 'I am the LORD, and there is none else.'" More frequently than not, God includes a co-relational message to man when describing the created beauty of His flora and fauna. Notice, God created the earth for man's habitation. Let us combine our consideration of man and all living creatures in this next portion along with the edicts that God gave on Creation's Day Six. The question is, Where has God taken us? And where are we going?

First God formed the land, and then vegetation, fish, birds, assorted insects, and on Day Six, cattle, creeping things and various creatures, culminating in mankind. We are all together in this big celestial soup of planet earth when one considers we are all a part of God's entire creation including the sun, moon and stars, and the entire universe. Just how did God make our planet and environment habitable for mankind within six days? He did it by placing man in a beautiful garden which we know today as the Garden of Eden. As growth occurred each day, according to God's edicts, the earth became more compatible to man and to his hands to cultivate and care for it. In some ways, the Garden of Eden might be comparable to a womb, a place for temporary growth. Adam and Eve were being weaned as the earth was rapidly being prepared by God, and His angels, for man's habitation. The time of man's fall from grace was sometime after Creation's Day Six.

Yet even in their fallen state, God loved humans and made everything to give them joy. He created everything to fit into a certain specified niche in His established ecosystems, everything from the lowly mouse scrambling along the ground eating seeds, to spores and probably some insects, necessary for the development and control of the ecosystems under the firmament's canopy. We see the giraffe, at the top of the ecosystem, eating leaves high in the trees in a niche unoccupied by other animals on our earth. Look at the American bison, not built like the giraffe, yet at times occupying a similar niche to the giraffe, yet in some respects in a different life system. The bison also ate the tops of trees on the plains as they browsed over small trees and ate the leaves and twigs passing under their bellies as they walked. Many birds, monkeys, lemurs and numerous other created creatures similarly browsed the upper canopy of trees fitting into the respective environmental niche where God placed them.

In contrast, man's niche in this ecosystem is one of management assigned by God to create a pristine beauty on earth to be lived in by his descendants until time for the new heaven and earth. In His great wisdom, God has given us good things to do while we live here on earth in our fallen state. Stewardship applies to everything God has entrusted to us. It is not restricted to nature only, but to all things that God has given us, including, family, friends, wealth, health, and material items, anything that God has entrusted us with.

Within man's niche, God gives us work to do with gladness of heart in peace and salvation. Psalms 24:1 says, "The earth is the LORD'S, and all it contains, the world, and those who dwell in it." Psalms 90:14-17 adds, [14]"O satisfy us in the morning with Your lovingkindness, that we may sing for joy and be glad all our days. [15]Make us glad according to the days You have afflicted us, *and* the years we have seen evil. [16]Let Your work appear to Your servants and Your majesty to their children. [17]Let the favor of the Lord our God be upon us; and confirm for us the work of our hands; yes, confirm the work of our hands." Isaiah 52:7 says, [7]"How lovely on the mountains are the feet of him who brings good news, who announces peace and brings good news of happiness, who announces salvation, *and* says to Zion, 'Your God reigns!'"

Whether the work God assigns to us individually is the work of our hands, or the work of a scribe, it is all to be "Kingdom" work done for the glory of God. Therefore, the daily work we do will bring joy and gladness. We can count on the Bible's promises for doing all "to the glory of God." Christ reigns. He is immortal, invisible, most Holy God, and He reigns in the lives of His people. For this reason we go forward, under His guidance, and supported by His Holy Word. Perhaps our work, while we live on earth, is to present

His word not only through the Bible, but also through that written in our hearts. Our work may be to declare this to friend and foe alike, wherever God places us in the world. Yielding to that calling, the dreams God places in our minds and hearts are ones of peace, love, and a future filled with the joy of His being in all that He finds for us to do.

The beauty of the earth filled with God's amazing creatures is expressed poetically throughout scripture. Psalms 121:1-2 declares, [1]"I will lift up my eyes to the mountains; from whence shall my help come? [2]My help *comes* from the LORD, who made heaven and earth." Let's look up and fill our hearts with gladness by studying God's Holy Word to see just what is on these mountains, and how God's love presents it to mankind.

Psalms 18:31-33 says, [31]"For who is God, but the LORD? And who is a rock, except our God, [32]The God who girds me with strength and makes my way blameless? [33]He makes my feet like hinds' *feet,* and sets me upon my high places." Job 39:1-2 adds, [1]"Do you know the time the mountain goats give birth? Do you observe the calving of the deer? [2]Can you count the months they fulfill, or do you know the time they give birth?" Similarly, consider Psalms 104:18, "The high mountains are for the wild goats; the cliffs are a refuge for the shephanim (Coney, or small rabbit-like mountain creature). Isaiah 40:31"Yet those who wait for the LORD will gain new strength; they will mount up *with* wings like eagles, they will run and not get tired, they will walk and not become weary."

God's inspired poetry shines forth in creative beauty in the above scriptures concerning the animals in His kingdom being placed in various locations in nature for mankind to care for, nourish and be nourished by in return. In the above passages, his creative beauty isn't limited just to the well being of created animals, but also contains blessed promises for the men and women to whom He has assigned their care. For humankind, God provides the distribution of the food, wealth, health and habitation in the form of clothing and housing for work done for the Kingdom's sake while we live on this earth. In 1 Corinthians 9:9-10, God describes how He provides for all of our needs: [9]"For it is written in the Law of Moses, "You shall not muzzle the ox while he is threshing." God is not concerned about oxen, is He? [10]Or is He speaking altogether for our sake? Yes, for our sake it was written, because the plowman ought to plow in hope, and the thresher *to thresh* in hope of sharing *the crops.*"

This scripture indicates that we, as human workers, are entitled to our share of the harvest, earned sustenance for our labors. If we are working for a dairy farmer, shoveling manure in another man's barn, that payment should be received from the farmer we are working for in a manner to sufficiently feed and care for ourselves and our household, whether it is by monetary reward or material products such as: milk, cheese, meat, flour, etc. Whatever beneficial and productive work our hands find to do, as we live on earth, we are to do with all of our hearts as unto the Lord.

Consider the small things in God's creation that make our hearts glad: Matthew 6:27-30 [27]"And who of you by being worried can add a *single* hour to his life? [28]And why are you worried about clothing? Observe how the lilies of the field grow; they do not toil nor do they spin, [29]yet I say to you that not even Solomon in all his glory clothed himself like one of these. [30]But if God so clothes the grass of the field, which is *alive* today and tomorrow is thrown into the furnace, *will He* not much more *clothe* you? You of little faith!" In the Beatitudes, Jesus shows that vegetative food is provided for all of God's created beings, and also shows us the beauty of the simplest things in His creation. He further points out man's general lack of faith in what He has provided for our sustenance for both us and for all of His created beings. On the Creation's Day Six, God provided vegetation for all of His creatures, for us to eat, and be glad (Genesis 1:29-30).

After the flood, God added to man's diet, but with restrictions: Genesis 9:3-7, [3]"'Every moving thing that is alive shall be food for you; I give all to you, as *I gave* the green plant. [4]Only you shall not eat flesh with its life, *that is,* its blood. [5]Surely I will require your lifeblood; from every beast I will require it. And from *every* man, from every man's brother I will require the life of man. [6]Whoever sheds man's blood, by man his blood shall be shed, for in the image of God He made man. [7]As for you, be fruitful and multiply; populate the earth abundantly and multiply in it.'"

During the course of Israel's history, specific menu restrictions were made to assure dietary health. For example, man was not allowed to eat unclean animals. These food laws for proper hygiene protected God's people from improper cooking, handling and ingestion of certain foods harmful to humanity, such as vultures, hawks, crows, etc., known to eat dead animals and therefore carry in and on their flesh potential diseases that seriously threaten mankind. Additional dietary restrictions were made concerning swine and animals with differing habits of ingestion important to their specific niche in the environment, but whose God-given role requirements caused them to live in unclean habitat. However, not all animals classified as unclean and detrimental to mankind by dietary laws were restricted simply for health reasons. Consider the rabbit, a food common in all cultures, yet labeled unclean in Old Testament scriptures for reasons known only to God's wisdom, rather than being for any obvious health issue we can ascertain today.

In the New Testament as compared to the Old, we see God change required eating habits for Kingdom purposes. We do not fully comprehend God's New Testament edict abolishing many, but not all, of the health laws He gave ages ago. Here is an example of God lifting His ancient edict through the vision given to Peter in Acts 11:7-10: [7]"I also heard a voice saying to me, 'Get up, Peter; kill and eat.' [8]But I said, 'By no means, Lord, for nothing unholy or unclean has ever entered my mouth.' [9]But a voice from heaven answered a second time, 'What God has cleansed, no longer consider unholy.' [10]This happened three times, and everything was drawn back up into the sky."

In this instance, God was not just discussing diet with Peter for the sake of the Jewish people, but also for the ministry of Christ to the whole world, both Jews and Gentiles. This is also seen in Acts 15:19-21: [19]"Therefore it is my judgment that we do not trouble those who are turning to God from among the Gentiles, [20]but that we write to them that they abstain from things contaminated by idols and from fornication and from what is strangled and from blood. [21]For Moses from ancient generations has in every city those who preach him, since he is read in the synagogues every Sabbath."

God is not restrictive to the Jews for dietary purposes, but non-restrictive to the Gentiles except for the restrictions held in regards to weaker brothers, who in this case happened to be Jewish converts. Most people today have some knowledge of basic Jewish dietary laws and practices. Generally, the Gentiles ate everything from both clean and unclean animals, contrary to the beliefs and practices of the Jews. Yet here God tells Peter that it is now okay for the Gentiles to eat as they had in the past, without dietary restrictions—that what is eaten is not condemning to their faith. Meanwhile, the Church *was* told to restrict some eating habits so as not to stumble or repulse weaker brothers, meaning Jews who refrained from eating specified foods, or blood, or things strangled or sacrificed to idols, according to their ancient beliefs.

Now let us compare God-given Jewish food laws to some perhaps parallel practices within the Native American heritage. Prior to the arrival of people from foreign lands reaching North American shores, the Indian peoples were food gatherers. Early Native American life consisted of hunting, fishing, and gathering herbs, vegetables, fruit and whatever the land provided. And they did this without harming the environment in any permanent way that we can detect today. Due to the predominantly continental climate in the Americas, life necessitated storing foods for use during the unproductive fall, winter and spring seasons. This entailed drying, smoking, and in some cases freezing foods for preservation during the months that food was unavailable for daily gathering. Otherwise, Native Americans lived off of the land in harmony with nature. Perhaps they were the original Conservationists.

However, sources within the Native American culture tell me that prior to the coming of modern man, Indian people also were acquainted with jealousy and greed as exhibited in raiding war parties into the neighboring tribes. Therefore the white man is not totally responsible for bringing humanity's worst into the world of the original Americans. Since the fall of mankind in the Garden of Eden, man's heart has been considerably wicked and evil so that not even relatively isolated Native Americans were exempt from this inherited malady. Scripture says that all of us like sheep have gone astray from the path that God destined for humanity.

Historically, Native Americans have had admirable ways of dealing with their natural livelihood. They generally gathered no more than what they needed for their life in the near future. They took no more than their essentials and gathered it in thankfulness and prayer. Their example is one of stewardship by need, not greed. Their conduct is parallel to that set forth in the Bible for God's chosen people, the Jews. In the wilderness, His people had to trust in God for their daily sustenance. God trained them to do so by arranging that any excess manna gathered would rot the next day unless that following day was the week's seventh day of rest when man was not to labor. On the sixth day only, God decreed that the extra manna gathered for the seventh day of rest would not spoil.

Early humanity, both the Jewish and Native American people, enjoyed the thrill of the hunt and the taste for wild game described in such Bible stories as the hunter, Nimrod, with his love for wild game. That theme is also portrayed in the account of the patriarch, Isaac, and his hunter son, Esau. In the Bible, God says that we will be held responsible for what we take from nature. As good conservationist stewards of the land, we have a hereditary standard for working with nature. My hope is that those who love the land that our God created will help train others in our world to live and care for it as dedicated stewards.

Truthfully, good stewardship is needed for all facets of life and work that we find ourselves involved in as long as God allows us to live on this planet. But if the Lord tarries, perhaps we can steward and prepare our environment as an acceptable love gift back to the Lord of Lords and King of Kings when He returns. To accomplish this task properly will require all citizens of our world obeying God's laws and principles and practicing good stewardship in all things, now and forevermore.

God created cows, horses, pigs and sheep,
Different kinds given us to keep.
Lions, tigers, bears and wolves,
All created for our good.

Things were created that fly, creep and crawl,
But man alone was made to stand tall,
Endowed with wisdom to maintain,
All life on earth ours to sustain.

Chapter 11

GOD'S REST:
CREATION'S DAY SEVEN

There is a place of quiet rest near to the heart of god;
A place where sin does not molest; near to the heart of god.

The above lines are from the famous hymn of the same name by Cleland B. McAfee. Other words concerning rest, like "May you rest in peace," may seem like an ominous statement heard at the bedside of loved ones sick unto death, or at a graveside. Yet the phrase, "Rest in peace," should bring comfort and joy to all who labor and are heavy laden in this life. Physical and spiritual rest are both a gift from God to those who hear the Lord's call in our lives. It is His divine reward.

The Bible's first mention of rest appears in Genesis 2:1-2, [1]Thus the heavens and the earth were completed, and all their hosts. [2]By the seventh day God completed His work which He had done, and He rested on the seventh day from all His work which He had done. [3]Then God blessed the seventh day and sanctified it, because in it He rested from all His work which God had created and made." In Genesis 1:31, at the end of the sixth day of creation we are told, "God saw all that He had made and behold, it was very good."

After six days of work, God rested. Yet what an amazing six days those were! During them God gave us all that we know and observe in this world with our senses, plus the perceptions that occur in our minds, whether good or bad. To date our eternal Father has not given us the depth of knowledge or wisdom to fully perceive all of His planning work that went into Him setting up the cosmos for this great event, eternity. As humans, we cannot fathom the timelessness of eternity, or what God was doing before He created us, since our existence is finite and limited to our human perception. Modern man may think we are quite smart with our computers, spaceships and marvelous communication devices. However, we cannot yet find solutions to correct pollution or the destruction of our environment, for which we are largely guilty.

This world, that God declared *very good*, is not currently the garden spot that He created. Tares, or weeds, have taken hold of nature as well as of our personal lives during the millenniums in between. Yet throughout history God mercifully declares in His Bible that when we call upon Him in repentance and turn from our evil ways, He will restore our lives and the land we live in to the blessed pristine beauty and habitation He originally provided for all humanity. This may not occur as we might wish in the twinkling of an eye, but may require cheerful hard work by those God appoints for such tasks in preparing this world for the return of His Son. Even discussing this prospect may seem like a pleasant dream versus the hard face of reality of a world gone amuck. But let us agree with John the Baptist, "Repent for the kingdom of God is at hand," and say as He later quotes from the words of Isaiah, "Prepare ye the way of the Lord."

On God's seventh day, He rested. But before He rested, until mankind's "fall," He declared that everything that He had made was "very good." When Genesis tells us that on the seventh God rested from all of His labors, it does not mean He went into oblivion for that period. Instead His rest was more like that described in Psalms 121:1-4: [1]"I will lift up my eyes to the mountains; from whence shall my help come? [2]My help *comes* from the LORD, who made heaven and earth. [3]He will not allow your foot to slip; He who keeps you will not slumber. [4]Behold, He who keeps Israel will neither slumber nor sleep." The psalmist here declares that God is aware at all times and on every occasion. Psalms 121:7-8 says, [7]"The LORD will protect you from all evil; He will keep your soul. [8]The LORD will guard your going out and your coming in from this time forth and forever. Isaiah 37:28 adds words of comfort: 'But I know your sitting down and your going out and your coming in and your raging against Me."

In each of these scriptures we see that although God is aware of our situations at all times, it may not always seem that way to us. For example, Psalms 44:22-23 says: [22]"But for Your sake we are killed all day long; we are considered as sheep to be slaughtered. [23]Arouse Yourself, why do You sleep, O Lord? Awake, do not reject us forever."

It interests me that although God rests, He does not sleep. We cannot ascribe human qualities to God in order to make them sensible to our human understanding. To do so is called *personification* or *anthropomorphism,* attributing animistic or human qualities to an object that is not animist or human, in this case, our loving but divine God. The concept of seeing God sleeping or resting like any of us is an attribute beyond the understanding of our finite minds. Yet according to the seventh day of creation, He did enter into some kind of divine rest.

In many places in scripture, God commands a Sabbath rest for mankind. Consider Deuteronomy 5:12-15, [12]'Observe the Sabbath day to keep it holy, as the LORD your God commanded you. [13]'Six days you shall labor and do all your work, [14]but the seventh day is a Sabbath of the LORD your God; *in it* you shall not do any work, you or your son or your daughter or your male servant or your female servant or your ox or your donkey or any of your cattle or your sojourner who stays with you, so that your male servant and your female servant may rest as well as you. [15]'You shall remember that you were a slave in the land of Egypt, and the LORD your God brought you out of there by a mighty hand and by an outstretched arm; therefore the LORD your God commanded you to observe the Sabbath day.'"

Humans need rest from their labors in order to function. During the French Revolution, reformers briefly redesigned the calendar into ten-day weeks of nine work days and one day of rest. However, physicians and leaders soon reported that this pattern was not good for the human body or mind. The divine pattern God gave is work six days; rest one. I have a good doctor, who knows my general physical/emotional history. My doctor orders me to rest on a weekly basis with the following mandate, "God created the heavens and earth in six days and rested on the seventh. God intends that you also rest on the seventh day from your labor. This does not mean that you can work six eighteen hour days and then rest. It means to be sensible and set aside one day of the week to rest body, mind and soul." I personally believe that a true rest should include a God-rest in a church, hopefully including worship and fellowship with fellow believers.

In the beginning, prior to man's fall into sin, Adam and Eve lived in a state of rest with God in the beautiful Garden of Eden. They also had the mandate to work, for God told them to be fruitful and multiply and take care of the earth and all that it contained, but they were at peace with Him and living in harmony with all of creation. Then, bang, along came the deceiver and Adam and Eve's subsequent fall. They, and consequently all of mankind, had to be cast out of the garden and into the world to obtain their food by hard labor with the sweat of their brow while separated from God's presence. This was done for their protection and that of their descendents so that their fallen state would not become eternal. However, immediately our loving God began speaking words concerning the promise of a redeeming Savior, and that certainty was passed on to every generation until it was fulfilled with the coming of Jesus Christ millenniums later.

According to most studies in science and scripture, the world before the fall was very different. Geological deposition indicates that many different flora and fauna existed during the pre-flood time. At the time of the flood, the whole world appears to have undergone dramatic change. This was predicted at Noah's birth by his father, Lamech, in Genesis 5:28-29 and pertains to rest: [28]"Lamech lived one hundred and eighty-two years, and became the father of a son. [29]Now he called his name Noah, saying, 'This one will give us rest from our work and from the toil of our hands *arising* from the ground which the LORD has cursed.'"

Many of the hardships portrayed in cave man stories and movies may not be too farfetched in concerning mankind's prehistoric days. Descriptions of dense, wet fern-laden jungles filled with awesome dinosaurs amidst varied flora and fauna species now extinct, may actually have been the case due to changes at the time of the flood. My understanding is that some semblance of rest occurred at the time of Noah with the end of the flood, and was given to mankind along with the new but imperfect creation we know today.

It seems clear that at this time God gave humankind some rest from their labors compared to the ceaseless labor required in the conditions prior to the flood. This *rest* is not a cessation of all labor, but does allow some recreational *time out* from the harsh conditions and into God's world of light.

Some people find a more complete *rest* in the realm of God than others. This *rest* is described in scripture with additional light shed through human observations and writings. Recall the common saying, that something is a "labor of love"? This describes tasks filled with the joys of daily living beneficial to God, self and mankind. This may be experienced by a happy farmer driving his tractor, a man caring faithfully for an invalid child or parent, or someone like me writing to benefit readers for a better life in Christ.

Although physical rest and God's rest are frequently intermingled as rewards and commands for our good, they are not synonymous. In the Old Testament, God commanded us to remember the seventh or Sabbath day to keep it holy and to rest from our labors. This spoke of physical rest only, if God was left out of the equation. But it means physical rest plus godly rest when incorporated with a day of communion with and worship of our Creator. Many outdoor enthusiasts tell me, "I worship God best with a fishing rod in my hand standing on the shore of one of God's pristine lakes here in Minnesota."

My answer is, "How strong is your meditation on your Creator when a big one bites?" I recall walking in the highlands overlooking Lake Superior singing praises in worship of our Lord for the entire hour it took me to return to the road and my car. Although this is excellent and good, something is still lacking. That is fellowship with other Christians. Hebrews 10:24-25 instructs, [24]"and let us consider how to stimulate one another to love and good deeds, [25]not forsaking our own assembling together, as is the habit of some, but encouraging *one another*; and all the more as you see the day drawing near."

Love is not blind, and it is best learned and accomplished in the presence of others. Love is also actions. Jesus expressed his love for the whole world, in front of the whole world, through His death on the cross. We also need to express our love for one another and to one another. For me, the best way to do this is in reverent fellowship systematically and periodically with other Christians at the meeting place of our choice. Remember the lines quoted from the popular hymn at the start of this chapter?

There is a place of quiet rest near to the heart of God;
A place where sin does not molest; near to the heart of God.

That's it! This song states the rest we all desire! We may look for it in many places, but have trouble finding true "God rest" at times. *God's rest* is found within us after examination and repentance to Him, and also from without by forgiveness, work and communion with Him. Hebrews 3:17-19 states the problem: [17]"And with whom was He angry for forty years? Was it not with those who sinned, whose bodies fell in the wilderness? [18]And to whom did He swear that they would not enter His rest, but to those who were disobedient? [19]*So* we see that they were not able to enter because of unbelief."

Belief and faith go hand in hand. In Mark 9:14-29, Jesus tells the father of a deaf mute that his son can be healed if the father will believe. In those verses, the man's response is, "I do believe, help my unbelief," and his child is healed. This common but effective prayer concerning unbelief is often heard in many circumstances due to our wavering faith. Martin Luther made famous use of this phrase found in both Old and New Testament scriptures, "The just shall live by faith." We must rely upon this, living by faith daily, even if we sometimes falter.

The other important point is to live in obedience to God. You might say, "That is easier said than done."

We might reply, "Practice makes perfect." The fact is that even if we are prone to fall in recurring or secret sin, do an about face, stop and remember, "Practice makes perfect."

Hebrews 4:1-11 urges us, [1]"Therefore, let us fear if, while a promise remains of entering His rest, any one of you may seem to have come short of it. [2]For indeed we have good news preached to us, just as they also; but the word they heard did not profit them, because it was not united by faith in those who heard. [3]For we who have believed enter that rest, just as He has said, 'As I swore in My wrath, they shall not enter My rest,' although His works were finished from the foundation of the world. [4]For He has said somewhere concerning the seventh *day*: 'And God rested on the seventh day from all His works,' [5]and again in this *passage*, 'They shall not enter my rest.' [6]Therefore, since it remains for some to enter it, and those who formerly had good news preached to them failed to enter because of disobedience, [7]He again fixes a certain day, 'Today,' saying through David after so long a time just as has been said before, 'Today if you hear His voice, do not harden your hearts.' [8]For if Joshua had given them rest, He would not have spoken of another day after that. [9]So there remains a Sabbath rest for the people of God. [10]For the one who has entered His rest has himself also rested from his works, as God did from His. [11]Therefore let us be diligent to enter that rest, so that no one will fall, through *following* the same example of disobedience."

In these verses it becomes obvious that we must act positively in faith, seeking release from our sinful nature to enter God's Sabbath rest as described on Creation's Day Seven. Although it may look like *mission impossible* at times, Jesus has led the way. He knows and shows us the proper way to enter God's rest. I recall a man visiting my church who was seeking the sanctuary. He appeared panic stricken just short minutes before the church service was to begin. After the service I saw this same man again and could visibly discern that in the meantime he had found God's rest in quiet meditation during service in God's house. He now appeared quietly at peace. Obtaining God's rest is easy. We go to Jesus and learn from Him and His Word. As Matthew 11:28-30 instructs, [28]"Come to Me, all who are weary and heavy-laden, and I will give you rest. [29]Take My yoke upon you and learn from Me, for I am gentle and humble in heart, and you will find rest for your souls. [30]For My yoke is easy and My burden is light.'"

We don't just read the Bible and then go our own way. We do it God's way, learning to walk with Him in the footsteps of Jesus. When this is accomplished, we find "rest for our souls." This rest isn't yet permanent for Christians on earth, but is our eternal promise once we become alive in Christ and trust in Him.

More explanation is given in John 10:7-10: [7]"So Jesus said to them again, 'Truly, truly, I say to you, I am the door of the sheep. [8]All who came before Me are thieves and robbers, but the sheep did not hear them. [9]I am the door; if anyone enters through Me, he will be saved, and will go in and out and find pasture. [10]The thief comes only to steal and kill and destroy; I came that they may have life, and have *it* abundantly.'"

The point is, clothed in God's presence, we are led in safety as we go in and out of places where He leads us. We are in this world, but not "of it." We are cared for and nurtured by our Lord while going forward as He wills and commands, while abiding in His rest.

True rest is physical rest as well as spiritual. Many people may obtain the physical rest of a weekend without going to church and fellowshipping with believers and thereby miss out on the God rest. Some of us may be required to work on Sundays. However, keeping the Sabbath day holy is not violated when a physical rest is instituted on another day with a God rest conducted at another time with believers in the faith. God's word says, "How can they hear without a preacher?" To grow in Christian faith requires someone to preach/teach on the day we can observe Sabbath rest without violating God's command. According to the words of Jesus in Mark 2:27, "The Sabbath was made for man and not man for the Sabbath." God has determined that a day must be set aside for physical rest. Hopefully, if possible, this day can also correspond on the seventh day God specified for rest. For most of us, this day of physical rest and God rest is Sunday. But no matter when we are able to observe it, we should seek to enter God's full unconditional rest.

God's rest also can be obtained while doing God's work. In Matthew 11:29-30, Jesus said: [29]"Take My yoke upon you and learn from Me, ... [30]For My yoke is easy and My burden is light." When studying, teaching, or preaching, we are co-sharing the yoke of Christ and pulling together with Him, regardless of the day of the week. Whether I preach, teach, or study, I am doing God work and obtaining His rest. Concerning their work, you sometimes hear people say, "It isn't work at all, but a labor of love." It is the same way with most born-again lovers of God and those working for him.

Some tasks can be quite hazardous, even fraught with danger to the point of costing a person's life as was the case with Martin Luther King, Jr. Yet he did not shirk the work set before him but followed the path set by God. Christ paved the way for all of us to His father's glory. We can be in God's rest while doing God's work, but require physical rest, too. Hopefully God will provide us peace while we do needed tasks, enabling us to incorporate physical rest with a day of

God rest at the same time. If you can't take a Sunday off from work, find another time during the week to obtain God rest and fellowship with other believers.

Remember appearances can be deceiving. Although at times it may seem that way, none of us are truly *Lone Rangers,* We need fellowship with others whenever possible. During the Vietnam War, when captured by the North Vietnamese, American military personnel developed a code to convey scripture to one another by tapping out code through their prison cell walls. Despite their broken bodies and mental anguish, the encouragement and communion provided through this communication kept many of them alive in spite of the terrible times that tried their very souls and sometimes took their lives.

Since the time of Jesus, Christians have been persecuted all over the world, often facing or experiencing death, without losing their faith. In our times and circumstances, most of us worship in comfort and peace whenever and wherever we choose. We should thank God for this every day. The way we as Christians can best survive is to live as one in Christ.

God never promised us an easy life, but we are never alone. If we have a good life in Christ, enjoy it with thanksgiving. If times get tough, don't give up, but take a lesson from our country's POW's. Fellow Christians are where we find them, and where God leads us. Some are in the trenches and others in beautiful pristine chapels. Wherever you find yourself, look to our Creator to please Him, praying for peace and understanding in a world gone into sinful violent opposition to Him. Seek the Lord our God in Christ, who paved the way for us to follow. He is open and willing to share our load, while we're in training, by sharing

His yoke with each of us.

Psalms 34:14-15 advises, [14]"Depart from evil and do good; seek peace and pursue it.[15]The eyes of the LORD are toward the righteous and His ears are *open* to their cry. Seek the Lord while He may be found, call upon Him while He is near." When we turn to the Lord in doing good He hears us, cleans us up, and brings us into His rest both on the seventh day, and whenever we need rest in mind, body and soul. In tumultuous times, go to one of the key scripture verses discussing God's rest. Carry your Bible or New Testament with you in your pocket or purse to ease your way into God's rest when you falter. His word will comfort you whatever your joy, pain or need. You will *rest in peace*, untroubled, while enjoying life here and now.

There is a peace that transcends minds,
Giving rest to all mankind,
Established by God from days of old,
A Sabbath rest to all, we're told.

Honor and respect the God who gives
Life to all on this planet who live.
Created by God on the seventh day,
He rested that all of us might say:

Glory to God in the highest;
We sing His praises all day.
Glory to God in the highest;
We worship Him and we pray.

Chapter 12

ABRAM AND POST-CREATION DAYS

"When the bow is in the cloud, then I will look upon it, to remember the everlasting covenant between God and every living creature of all flesh that is on the earth. GENESIS 9:16,

The creation days have ended,
The garden is now unattended.
The Humpty-Dumpty's have had their great fall,
And mankind now struggle to hear God's call.

Man's road back to recovery began immediately after his fall into sin and away from God. Our merciful Heavenly Father immediately gave the promise of a Savior and began divine steps towards its fulfillment. The full redemption process also includes rest from hard labor, the return from apostasy resulting from the Babel incident scattering inhabitants over the earth's surface, and the wonderful realization of man's restoration through Abraham's descendent (Christ), finally redeeming and preparing him to enter creation's new heavens and new earth. Let's look more closely at that promise.

The Genesis 3:1, 6, 13, record says, [1]"Now the serpent was more crafty than any beast of the field which the LORD God had made. And he said to the woman, 'Indeed, has God said, 'You shall not eat from any tree of the garden?'... [6]When the woman saw that the tree was good for food, and that it was a delight to the eyes, and that the tree was desirable to make *one* wise, she took from its fruit and ate; and she gave also to her husband with her, and he ate...[13]Then the LORD God said to the woman, 'What is this you have done?' And the woman said, 'The serpent deceived me, and I ate...'"

In response, so that Adam and Eve's now fallen imperfect condition did not become permanent and eternal, God made a choice making mankind's future redemption possible. Genesis 3:16-19, [16]"To the woman He said, 'I will greatly multiply your pain in childbirth, in pain you will bring forth children; yet your desire will be for your husband, and he will rule over you.' [17]Then to Adam He said, 'Because you have listened to the voice of your wife, and have eaten from the tree about which I commanded you, saying, You shall not eat from it; cursed is the ground because of you; in toil you will eat of it all the days of your life. [18]Both thorns and thistles it shall grow for you; and you will eat the plants of the field; [19]by the sweat of your face you will eat bread, till you return to the ground, because from it you were taken; for you are dust, and to dust you shall return.'"

In subsequent verses, God clearly began making important eternal promises. Genesis 3:14-15 says: [14]"The

LORD God said to the serpent, 'Because you have done this, cursed are you more than all cattle, and more than every beast of the field; on your belly you will go, and dust you will eat all the days of your life; [15]and I will put enmity between you and the woman, and between your seed and her seed; He shall bruise you on the head, and you shall bruise him on the heel.'"

In Genesis 3:20-23, God begins to make clear His future merciful acts to mankind: [20]"Now the man called his wife's name Eve, because she was the mother of all *the* living. [21]The LORD God made garments of skin for Adam and his wife, and clothed them. [22]Then the LORD God said, 'Behold, the man has become like one of Us, knowing good and evil; and now, he might stretch out his hand, and take also from the tree of life, and eat, and live forever'— [23]therefore the LORD God sent him out from the garden of Eden, to cultivate the ground from which he was taken." Genesis 4:1 adds, "Now the man had relations with his wife Eve, and she conceived and gave birth to Cain, and she said, 'I have gotten a manchild with *the help of* the LORD.'" Here Eve believes God has given her and Adam the redeemer in accordance with His promise. However, this would not occur until Christ's arrival nearly 4,000 years later.

Genesis 1-11 Dating

The following information is important to show the dating sequence according to the genealogy of key personage as related to the formation of our earth as we know it today. It also further establishes the time of the giving of God's covenant to Abram, or "Father Abraham," as we know him, through whom we are all descended and through whom we receive Judeo-Christian but also Arab beliefs and heritage. The following chart presents the Genealogy of Adam and even through Abram (later Abraham).

Ancestry	Creation Dated		Significant BC Dates	
	Birth	Death	Birth	Death
Adam & Eve	0	930	4000 BC	
Seth	130	1042		
Methuselah	687	1656 (Flood)		2300
Lamech	874	1651		
Noah	1056	2006	2900	1950
Peleg	1750 (+2)		2200	
Abram	1945 (+2)		2000	*(1825 BC)

* Dating: The creation dated list all derives from the, *NASB*, Zondervan; Grand Rapids, Michigan, 2002. The date of the death of Abraham is taken from, *New Bible Dictionary*: 2nd Edition, Tyndale House Publishers, Wheaton Illinois, 1982. These dates are listed to the nearest year as indicated in the Bible; however, there is evidence of some estimating concerning the years of birth around the time of the flood and perhaps some rounding. For example, Noah's descendants, Shem, Ham and Japheth, were probably not triplets born exactly five hundred years after Noah's birth. Also, the exact date of the flood appears to have begun right after the death of Methuselah, which may in fact have been the triggering point of this great event.

The (+2) noted above is a correction factor assuming that the flood date is more key than the apparently rounded birthdates of Shem and his descendant, Arpachshad, born two years after the flood. I am convinced of the inerrancy of the

Bible, but must acknowledge that its purpose is not to provide all detail necessary to calculate all natural historical details without a possible degree of error figure of + or − 2 years over the long periods of time extending from the creation of mankind.

Significantly, the common date terms BC for "Before Christ" and AD, understood to mean "After Death, are not found in or validated by the Bible. As explained at website http://www.gotquestions.org AD actually stands for the Latin phrase "Anno Domini" which means "in the year of our Lord." That site asks, "How could the year 1 BC have been 'before Christ' and 1 AD been 'after death'? Although BC does stand for Before Christ, the BC/AD dating system was actually "not fully implemented and accepted until several centuries after Jesus' death. The significant BC dates, current in use today, are approximated due to the lack of precision recording in the Bible from the generations since Abraham, as well as some variations noted in the first eleven chapters of Genesis."

The early chapters of Genesis relate the 1656 pre-flood years based on the generally-accepted flood date of 2300 BC. In short, on Creation's Day Three, God's word describes how He set the foundations of the earth into motion and created land forms as well as its varied vegetation cover. On Day Four, He created light in the form of the sun, moon and stars, giving rise to tidal fluctuations over the seas and providing the sunlight for plants to grow on earth's surfaces. On Day Five, water-borne life and birds began their life cycles and appeared in swarms, initiating the propagation of plant life through the aviary species along with the great calcareous deposit sequence of sedimentary rocks. On Day Six, God formed surface animal and reptile life, but His highest culminating event was the creation of man and woman in God's image. After six amazing creation days, God rested on Day Seven. Therefore, it is time to consider probable occurrences on the earth's surfaces until the birth of Abraham nearly two thousand years later (about 2000 BC). This estimation of the date for earth's creation, according to modern-day calendars, arrives at a creation date of around 4000 BC. At creation, God instructed mankind, "Be fruitful and multiply." Mankind has succeeded well in doing so, producing a world population currently just under seven billion people. However, man has been less successful in fulfilling God's accompanying instruction to rule the earth and subdue it. In the Garden of Eden experience, Adam and Eve experienced love, joy, peace and tranquility. But after they chose sin and fell, they lost their fellowship with God and encountered shame, pain, sickness, strife, war, and death. Their subsequent life involved hard labor, surviving by the sweat of their brow.

The Bible says little concerning earth's literal pre-flood history. The Bible is a spiritual book; scientific or geologic instruction is not its purpose. However, many accounts of a universal flood are known with common correlation amongst various tribes and people throughout the earth and have been passed on from generation to generation through millennia. The Bible records history through its genealogy records and possibly within the book of Job. In addition, the earth's physical geological record reveals some of the conditions that existed prior to the flood, although there is theorization as to explanations of those origins.

Life was rough and tough during pre-flood conditions

on earth, but God left mankind hope through the promise of a Savior. That promise was given to Eve, immediately after the fall, though not realized until the coming of Christ nearly four thousand years later. However, the great promise God gave mankind concerning redemption and restoration was never forgotten. That hope is evident even in the pre-flood song of Lamech on the birth of Noah in Genesis 5:29, 1056 years after creation: "Now he called his name Noah, saying, 'This one will give us rest from our work and from the toil of our hands *arising* from the ground which the LORD has cursed.'"

However, Noah did not rest. He worked to build the ark used to hold earth's terrestrial creatures from destruction by the torrents of water that would soon overwhelm the earth. Noah taught and preached words of warning and repentance as the true evangelists are doing today in the fallen world that we now live in. "Repent, for the kingdom of God is at hand," might have been the words of Noah during the century while he built the ark. These same words spoken by John the Baptist and then by Jesus have echoed throughout our world through the centuries and are still heard today. We must *take heed* lest we fail to listen and likewise perish in our sins as did the world of Noah's day except for him, his wife, and their three sons and their wives.

Profuse evil existing within both men and angels caused God much remorse and resulted in the flood to cleanse the earth. Consider Genesis 6:1-6: [1]"Now it came about, when men began to multiply on the face of the land, and daughters were born to them, [2]that the sons of God saw that the daughters of men were beautiful; and they took wives for themselves, whomever they chose. [3]Then the LORD said, 'My Spirit shall not strive with man forever, because he also is flesh; nevertheless his days shall be one hundred and twenty years.' [4]The Nephilim were on the earth in those days, and also afterward, when the sons of God came in to the daughters of men, and they bore *children* to them. Those were the mighty men who *were* of old, men of renown. [5]Then the LORD saw that the wickedness of man was great on the earth, and that every intent of the thoughts of his heart was only evil continually. [6]The LORD was sorry that He had made man on the earth, and He was grieved in His heart."

The Flood

Just imagine Noah's day and the observations and comments of people around him: "What is this? Where are all these animals coming from? Where are they going? Repent or perish? Do you think that what Noah said is true?" These must have been statements made and questions by people on earth during the days before Noah, his family and the animals entered the ark and God closed the door. Genesis 7:11-12 says, [11]In the six hundredth year of Noah's life, in the second month, on the seventeenth day of the month, on the same day all the fountains of the great deep burst open, and the floodgates of the sky were opened. [12]The rain fell upon the earth for forty days and forty nights."

The earth retched: Cells and lenses of water entrapped within earth's newly formed land mass exploded and gushed water from within because of the big squeeze when God applied pressure from within the earth. Pressure also occurred from above in the form of large water masses gathered for the great deluge upon earth. And then for forty days and nights the earth harshly convulsed, causing mountains to rise and fall and producing immense erosion on earth's young rock formations developed during the previous 1656 years. Mountains jutted upwards over 30,000 feet with valleys forming and reforming again and again as the earth convulsed under the tremendous pressures of rain and earthquakes. During the flood, shale and sandstone formed on a grand scale not seen since the days of creation, nor observed since. Finally silence came as the deluge ceased and the animals and eight people on board the ark sat back wondering what would occur next. Finally they felt a bump-bump as the ark rested upon Mount Ararat.

Five months passed as God re-gathered and removed the waters, so that dry land gradually returned. The landscape appeared quite different when Noah and his family emerged from the depths of the ark. The sun was brighter. The perpetual mist was gone. Clouds now formed by evaporation from the sun before falling again in a recurring cycle of more gentle rain. "Look in the sky!" the eight must have proclaimed as multi-colors formed the world's first rainbow before their eyes. Genesis 9:12-17 tells the story: [12]God said, "This is the sign of the covenant which I am making between Me and you and every living creature that is with you, for all successive generations; [13]I set My bow in the cloud, and it shall be for a sign of a covenant between Me and the earth. [14]It shall come about, when I bring a cloud over the earth, that the bow will be seen in the cloud, [15]and I will remember My covenant, which is between Me and you and every living creature of all flesh; and never again shall the water become a flood to destroy all flesh. [16]When the bow is in the cloud, then I will look upon it, to remember the everlasting covenant between God and every living creature of all flesh that is on the earth.' [17]And God said to Noah, 'This is the sign of the covenant which I have established between Me and all flesh that is on the earth.'"

When Noah and his family emerged from the ark in Genesis 9:7, they were given the same instructions for the post-flood resettlement of the earth that Adam and Eve had received 1656 years earlier: "As for you, be fruitful and multiply; Populate the earth abundantly and multiply in it." Although with this flood God had washed away earlier man's continual evil. Due to their fallen and as yet unredeemed natures, Noah and family perpetuated the same sin Eve had fallen into, desiring to be like God. Our world today demonstrates amazingly close parallels. Nevertheless, for them and us, God made a provision through the coming of Christ 2300 years after the flood for taking away the curse that had come upon all.

Later the people of Babel built a great tower to reach to the very heavens in their desire to be like God, yet without His holiness, wisdom and compassion. The Godhead of Father, Son and Holy Spirit had no choice but to thwart man's attempt to be one in heart and mind to usurp God's power by confusing their language so that they could no longer communicate readily between one another. Sometime after the flood, this resulting *babble*, or confusion of languages, caused those of similar tongue to venture out together in scattered destinations to the uttermost parts of the earth. The Bible describes mankind spreading over the face of the earth prior to the birth of Peleg, around 2200 BC, or 1750 years following creation.

The literal name, Peleg, like our modern version seen in *Earthquake McGoon* drawn by Al Capp in his wonderful cartoon strip, *Little Abner*" means "the time the lands were split and divided." At this time it seems certain that continental drift occurred, carrying away the different tribes, tongues and diversities of peoples we see throughout our world today. The people scattered by God, as a result of the Tower of Babel, gathered together in groups who spoke alike. As the earth was split, these separated groups were carried away with the movement of the continents. The significance of Peleg mentioned in the Bible is twofold: Genesis 10 and 1 Chronicles 1 both describe the earth being split at this time; Genesis 10 and 11, 1 Chronicles 1 and Luke 3 all list Peleg in the genealogy of our Lord, Jesus Christ.

The earth was quite young around 2200 BC when it split. This was around seventeen hundred years after creation. The earth's crust was still very fluid as were the newly formed depths of magma created by the intense pressures caused by the overburden weight of lands and seas. The earth fractured and split, carrying away the groups of like-minded people capable of communicating with each other following the Babel incident. Also carried away on the fractured pieces of mega-continent were the newly established communities of flora and fauna begun at creation. In time, cross-pollination within flora kinds resulted. Crossbreeding within kinds of fauna caused diversity through the segregation brought about by newly-separated continents. The species common to our world today thrived under the new climatic conditions formed under this new firmament with newly established seas and land topography completely different than the world had previously known.

Some species known under the old world establishment were destined for extinction because of their inability to survive in God's post-flood environment. Out went the dinosaurs and the animal and reptile forms not included by God in Noah's ark. Under the earth's new climatic conditions, most of the fern kinds of vegetation that grew under pre-flood hot house conditions ceased to thrive and grow. Instead, other vegetative species, which may have previously struggled amongst the jungle like growth canopy were released from previous mists into the glorious sunlight enabling them to survive and flourish as we see them now. Mankind was partially released from the curse of living hand to mouth by the sweat of his brow. He received greater rest from his labors when living by God's instruction, "six days shall thou labor and rest on the seventh." Doctors tell us that we rest well physically when we abide under these literal guidelines, and also spiritually when we abide by God's command, "Remember the Sabbath day to keep it holy," giving worship and praise to our Creator, Father, Son and Holy Spirit.

The Bible is detailed in providing genealogical records with plenty of *begats* to explain each generation. It also provides clear specific genealogy for God's Son, Jesus, fulfillment of God's most important promise, including such major figures as Noah to Peleg, to Abram, to David, to Jesus Christ.

Although Noah felt gratitude that God's instruction provided safety for his family and the animal pairs led to the ark, permitting their survival, he also felt overwhelming sadness at losing the many friends that did not listen to the warning of a coming flood in time to enter the ark.

After the flood in which God destroyed the world as man knew it, but rescued Noah and his family and the animals led to the ark, God promised that he would never again destroy the world by flood. He gave the rainbow as a beautiful visible token confirming that covenant promise. He does speak of the world having a later cleansing by fire, but again believing men and women who listen to God will be instructed and protected. Ultimately a new heaven and new earth will replace the old as foretold two-thousand years ago through both Old Testament prophets and New Testament writers. Much of that is described in the closing chapters of the Bible's last book, Revelation. In fact Revelation 11:15 makes plain that all believing Christians can look forward to the time when, "the *kingdoms of this world are become the kingdoms of our* Lord, and of his *Christ.*"

Along with Noah, it is our hope, and God's desire, for which He has made full provision, that none of us perish. Instead all may find new life through repentance and belief in the salvation available through trusting in God's Son, Jesus. Generally, clear Gospel teaching and the call to repentance is declared openly these days from most pulpits in most nations of the world. Sometimes it is declared with harsh, dire warnings concerning God's judgment including hell for those contradicting the laws of God and refusing salvation through Jesus. Other preachers emphasize God's great loving call of grace as evidenced through His Son's sacrifice on the cross, resurrection from the dead, and ascension into heaven. For those of us trusting in accepting new life through Jesus, Romans 8:29 tells us that, "those whom God foreknew, He also predestined to become conformed to the image of His Son, so that He would be the *firstborn* among *many brethren* " (including we who are born later into the *family of God).*

Whether the message proclaimed is one of condemnation or love, the message goes out into the world that our times are becoming much as they were in the days of Noah. Indeed, the words of Jesus to His disciples in Luke 17:22-27 are applicable for us today: [22]"The days will come when you will long to see one of the days of the Son of Man, and you will not see it. [23]They will say to you, 'Look there! Look here!' Do not go away, and do not run after *them.* [24]For just like the lightning, when it flashes out of one part of the sky, shines to the other part of the sky, so will the Son of Man be in His day. [25]But first He must suffer many things and be rejected by this generation. [26]And just as it happened in the days of Noah, so it will be also in the days of the Son of Man: [27]they were eating, they were drinking, they were marrying, they were being given in marriage, until the day that Noah entered the ark, and the flood came and destroyed them all." We live in very similar times.

As quoted earlier in Chapter 3, these lyrics to a once popular song said, "Those were the days, my friend; we thought they'd never end..." Only they did end. BE PREPARED!

It is time to consider the coming promise of a new heaven and earth as man returns to God and His righteousness. In 2 Peter 3:10-14, the Bible warns of condemnation for those who do not accept Him: [10]"But the day of the Lord will come like a thief, in which the heavens will pass away with a roar and the elements will be destroyed with intense heat, and the earth and its works will be burned up. [11]Since all these things are to be destroyed in this way, what sort of people ought you to be in holy conduct and godliness, [12]looking for and hastening the coming of the day of God, because of which the heavens will be destroyed by burning, and the elements will melt with intense heat! [13]But according to His promise we are looking for new heavens and a new earth, in which righteousness dwells. [14]Therefore, beloved, since you look for these things, be diligent to be found by Him in peace, spotless and blameless."

What should we do then as Christians today living on this planet? Bow our knees and pray that the clear Gospel message reaches all of mankind so that they will know God and be saved from the judgments at the end of this age. When will this occur? No one knows for sure, only God the Father. Perhaps if all those who call on His name turn to Him in repentance, an extension of His grace may be granted as it was to past generations in the days of Abraham. In the meantime, Hebrews 10:25 encourages us to not forsake "our own assembling together, as is the habit of some, but encouraging *one another*; and all the more as you see the day drawing near."

The rainbow sings within its rings,
Proclaiming peace on earth.
He calms the storms in the reborn,
To those given second birth.

May the morning star rise in your heart,
As God's truth is being proclaimed.
Christ has won as God's risen Son,
His kingdom children reign.

EPILOGUE

Creation's Glorious Story takes form and visible life on Creation's Day Three when the process of the formation of the rocks and minerals begins in our earth. This was most likely a precipitous formation of the land masses observable by us today in somewhat altered formations. Also during Creation's Day Three, God established the vegetative coverings for the earth after their kind, forming all that we observe on earth today. That vegetative cover includes what is now growing on the surface of the earth and that is seen in the geological record through many horizons of rock formations. With our inquisitive minds, mankind investigates these natural phenomena in order to understand more of our life here on earth and to read and understand the signature of our Creator, God. Indeed, He reveals Himself through all that He has created, which includes His spoken and written word in the Bible.

The glories of creation by the Father, Son and Holy Spirit have always enticed the minds of man to see more of His glory in the Bible, in poetry or inspired narrations of His creative beauty created by those who love Him. Deuteronomy 29:29 tells us, "The secret things belong to the LORD our God, but the things revealed belong to us and to our sons forever, that we may observe all the words of this law." By His law He established the heavens and the earth.

Hopefully, the words and spirit of this book have touched and inspired you. May God the Father, Son, and Holy Spirit continue to draw men and women into the wonders of His universe, world and very being to look and listen to the full and wondrous sounds of *Creation's Glorious Story*.

Sonshine, Earthshine and the Stars

The creation days have ended;
God's Son has since descended.
He suffered and died that we might arise;
With Him to the glories of the skies.

His kingdom is eternal;
The heavens are His journal.
Look to the skies, you cannot deny,
The stars declare His enterprise.

The firmament declares His beauty,
Sustained through His life and duty.
The clouds above His earth sustained
By His wisdom and holy name.

The majesty of cedar and pine
He planted on this earth so kind,
Planted for all humanity to use and see
His love when we act intelligently.

The earth we walk upon
Gives life to all His sons.
We live and grow by what we eat
When fed by words at Jesus' feet.

God lives in the oceans deep
Created for life to keep.
The waves above, the quiet below,
His storms of life will calm the soul.

God's Son is here to stay,
He will not leave or forsake us, you say.
God's work is true He lives through you,
When you love and trust and obey.

BIBLIOGRAPHY

Baker, Robert H. An Introduction to Astronomy; 6ᵗʰ Ed. Princeton, NJ: D. Van Nostrand Co., Inc. 1961.

Barbour, Ian G. Religion and Science. New York: Harper Collins Publishers.1997.

Cagan, C.L., Dr., with Robert Hymers. From Darwin to Design. New Kensington, PA: Whitaker House. 2006.

DeYoung, Don. Geology and Creation, Reader Series #5, Creation Research Society. 2004.

Epp, Theodore H. The God of Creation. Lincoln, NE: Back to the Bible Publishing. 1981.

Kemp, James F., Kemp's Handbook of Rocks, 6ᵗʰ ed. Lancaster, PA: Lancaster Press, Inc. 2007.

LaRocco, Chris, and Blair Rothstein. "The Big Bang: It sure was BIG!!" ww.umich.edu/~gs265/bigbang. htm

Morris, Henry M. The Genesis Record. Grand Rapids, MI: Baker Book House. 2006.

Stambaugh, James."The Days of Creation: A Semantic Approach." TJ Archive, Vol. 5, Issue 1, April 1991. Also available on the internet at www. answersingenesis.org

Taylor, Paul F. The Six Days of Genesis. Green Forest, AR: Master Books, Inc. 2007.

Thompson, Frank Charles, D.D., Ph.D. The Thompson Chain Reference Bible, New American Standard. Indianapolis: Kirkbride Bible Co. Inc. 1993.

Wikipedia, "History of the Big Bang Theory...The Big Bang "Never Happened," 1991; en.wikipedia.org/wiki/Big_Bang.

Wikipedia, "The Gap Theory...," 1991; en.wikipedia.org/wiki/Gap Theory

A friend loves at all times,
And a brother is born for adversity.
-Proverbs 17:17

Rejoice in the Lord with me!
-Exodus 15:2

God's Love in Christ

Don Douglat